TRAVEL

26

Editor: Bill Buford
Assistant Editor: Tim Adams
Commissioning Editor: Lucretia Stewart
Managing Editor: Angus MacKinnon
Assistant to the Editor: Jean Marray
Editorial Assistants: Tania Rice, Alicja Kobiernicka

Publisher/Consultant: Alice Rose George
Associate Publisher: Piers Spence
Financial Manager: Monica McStay
Subscriptions: Gillian Kemp, Imogen Ridler
Advertising and Circulation: Alison Ormerod

Contributing Editor: Todd McEwen
Picture Research: Lynda Marshall
Design: Chris Hyde
Executive Editor: Pete de Bolla
US Associate Publisher: Anne Kinard, Granta, 250 West 57th Street, Suite 1316, New York, NY 10107.

Editorial and Subscription Correspondence: Granta, 44a Hobson Street, Cambridge CB1 1NL. Telephone: (0223) 315290.
All manuscripts are welcome but must be accompanied by a stamped, self-addressed envelope or they cannot be returned.

Subscriptions: £16.00 for four issues. Overseas add £4 postage.

Granta is photoset by Hobson Street Studio Ltd, Cambridge, England, and printed by Hazell Watson and Viney Ltd, Aylesbury, Bucks.

Granta is published by Granta Publications Ltd and distributed by Penguin Books Ltd, Harmondsworth, Middlesex, England; Viking Penguin Inc., 40 West 23rd St, New York, New York, USA; Penguin Books Australia Ltd, Ringwood, Victoria, Australia; Penguin Books Canada Ltd, 2801 John Street, Markham, Ontario, Canada L3R 1B4; Penguin Books (NZ) Ltd, 182–90 Wairau Road, Auckland 10, New Zealand. This selection copyright © 1989 by Granta Publications Ltd.

Cover photograph by Eric Meola (The Image Bank).

Granta 26, Spring 1989

ISBN 014-01-2355-5

SUPPORTED BY THE
EASTERN
Arts

CONTENTS

RYSZARD
KAPUŚCIŃSKI
CHRISTMAS EVE
IN UGANDA

In the morning, I went to the market, thinking that perhaps they might be selling fish. As I was driving down an empty street I spotted a green Land Rover behind me. It disappeared, but a minute later it was there again, and as it overtook me I caught a glimpse of Amin bent over the steering wheel. The Land Rover sped on ahead, passing a crossroads, where I lost sight of it. Even so, I swear I could actually hear him—could hear his laughter in fact, receding, just audible. Shortly after I came up behind a convoy of vehicles, moving slowly—open Jeeps and soldiers, all in helmets, aiming their rifles into the trees as they passed them. In the middle of the convoy I noticed Amin's shiny Citroën-Maserati and on the back seat there was the massive figure of an officer who I could tell had been shot—caught, no doubt, by a sniper.

In driving behind the convoy, I wanted to be very inconspicuous. In fact, from the moment I spotted Amin, I made a point of neither accelerating nor slowing down—no turning or stopping. It's a well-known tactic: not to draw attention to yourself, to shrink to the size of a drop and sink into the ground. The eyes of these people are fixed, looking through the sights of their rifles, looking for a victim. In killing they seem to find an outlet, some kind of confirmation.

After some time—it seemed a frightfully long time—the convoy turned towards Naguru and I drove down to Kisenyi.

The reason I thought of buying fish was because it was Christmas Eve, and on Christmas Eve fish is the traditional supper in Poland. The idea was perhaps a little eccentric, but was one of a number of different tricks I kept trying to help me get by—to keep my mind intact. For that, you needed normality, a kind of ordinariness; you had to make yourself do the obvious things. As long as I can remember there had always been a golden brown, pungent fish on the table at supper on Christmas Eve. This alone accounted for my early morning expedition to the market in Kisenyi.

Kisenyi is the African heart of Kampala, an old crowded district, a city within a city. I used to walk around it dumbfounded by its improbably sharp colours and bewildering contrasts. I wandered, dazed, assaulted by a hundred strange, choking smells.

Photo: Popperfoto

Idi Amin.

The district existed in a state of incessant excitement—restless, unaccustomed to sleep. In Kisenyi, people bustled round the clock, trading into the evenings, when the bars, decked out in crinkled paper, would fill up and the drinking would begin. There would be dancing and seduction; old scores between tribes would be paid and repaid relentlessly. In Kisenyi, you could buy anything at any time—in the small Indian shops or from the countless vendors circling around you. And then in the thousands of booths run by witch-doctors, soothsayers and magicians, you might lose everything. It was an exuberant world, magical and unique—a buzzing world whose orbit was somewhat crazy and unpredictable.

But now Kisenyi had lost its magic, its old deceitful charm, and had become gloomy, suspicious and aggressive. I came here apprehensive, unsure of what might happen. Walking down the street you might suddenly be hit in the face with a stone; you might be beaten, have your arms twisted violently behind your back; you might be robbed of everything. There were ferocious gangs: there were people trying to start a quarrel, looking for trouble.

Sometimes a few whites (only a few remained) came to Kisenyi, hoping to buy something to eat. I met Padre Eusebio who came from the north where his mission had been burnt down and he had barely escaped with his life. I invited him to my Christmas Eve supper, gave him my address and directions. He took it all down and disappeared swiftly. Whites prefer not to talk in public places, not to gather in groups—a group arouses suspicions. Why are they standing here? What are they talking about? Who are they? Names. Addresses. Statements.

The market square: the heart of Kisenyi lost its colour a long time ago. Empty, broken-up stalls. Splintered boxes, torn sacks, bags. All over the enormous square there were bits of paper scattered by children and the wind. In the corner of the market, a few women had spread their wares on old sheets that were faded and worn—some tomatoes, bananas, nuts, eggs, which, a moment later, were all gone, stolen, grabbed up, amid people shouting and knocking each other on the head. Shortly, I would see the same people milling around the square, bored, aimless, waiting for a friend, or waiting to rob someone, or perhaps just waiting.

I thought of going home when the street that led to Lake Victoria suddenly resounded with the screams and shouts of children—lively, high-pitched voices that were at first distant and muffled, and then, as they approached, united into a rhythmic, joyful choir. I looked in its direction: a flock of barefooted, bedraggled children was running towards us, dancing, singing and clapping. In a second everyone woke up, became animated, interested. The procession, swinging back and forth in high spirits, marched into the square, chanting intently: 'They've caught a fish! They've caught a fish!'

A lorry appeared, dripping with water as if it had just emerged from the bottom of the lake and stopped amid the empty stalls that, now rusty, had once buckled under baskets of fish, shrimps, cephalopods and all manner of tangled and menacing heaps of *frutti di mare*. The fishy smell still lingered there. A few half-naked fishermen jumped down and, pushing back the gaping spectators, began to grapple with the gate at the back of the lorry. When they finally managed to unlock and let it down, we saw, on the bottom of the flat-bed, a surprisingly large, fat fish. Its silver spine was covered by patches of seaweed and it had a white-grey, squabby stomach. It still had some signs of life, its mouth composing itself into a monstrous, inscrutable, moustached smile.

I thought that the crowd which immediately surrounded the lorry would burst out shouting and cheering and demand that the fish be cut up quickly, divided and sold (indeed, the fishermen started taking out axes and knives). But I was wrong—a deep silence fell over the square. I didn't know what had happened; I glanced at the people standing round, at their black faces shining in the sun, composed, even tense. They stood, their eyes gazing intently at the fish, glittering, immobile, big as a mountain is big. They stood, staring at it, pondering how fat it was, how gigantic. Then someone in the crowd broke the silence. 'Port Bell?'

One of the fishermen, straightening his back, replied: 'Port Bell.'

They were terrible words, and a murmur passed over the square. Port Bell is one of the places where the torturers throw the bodies of those they've murdered; the lake where, after a night of terror, there is a floating cemetery, and where, afterwards, the fish feed.

13

In the silence that fell over the square everybody scrutinized the fish again as if, from its size, we might be able to deduce whether or not acts of repression were on the increase. We then heard the whine of an approaching lorry. An army squad was coming, attracted and made curious by the crowd that was filling and loitering around the square. Everybody was afraid of the soldiers, but there was nowhere to run; we could only stand and wait for whatever was going to happen. They arrived, jumped off their lorry and started towards the fishermen who, by now, were completely petrified.

The soldiers saw the fish. They liked it. They took a good look at it from all sides, nodded in approval and patted their bellies. They called over their driver, who then pulled up to the stall. We watched the fishermen who, prodded along by rifle-butts, loaded the fish into the lorry. It kept slipping away, trying to fight, but was at last pushed deep into the back of the lorry. Then, suddenly, the people standing close to the lorry cried out. As the fish was pushed inside, the soldiers pulled out a corpse spattered with blood. We stared at it, wondering where the corpse was being taken—perhaps to be sold back to the family; trading in dead bodies was profitable—when it was dumped on the table that was still streaming with water.

They started to leave.

It was almost noon, already quite hot. The crowd stood dumbfounded and silent. Gradually it stirred. The square began to empty.

I drove back home the same way as I had come. As I passed the road to Naguru, I met Amin's convoy just as I had that morning, as if it had never moved, not knowing what to do next, or where to go.

Home was a flat on the first floor of a typical colonial villa. Nobody had lived on the ground floor since the Indians had been kicked out, although sometimes I would hear whispers, knocking, even loud voices. I did not know who was making himself heard.

The flat had four rooms: two unfurnished—I never looked in them. In the third room there was a large, rickety bed with a mosquito net that was pitched like a tent and full of holes. Whenever the mosquitoes or my burdensome tapeworm (I couldn't get rid of it) allowed me, I slept there. The fourth room was the largest but also the emptiest. It had only one big table and two benches. The table was eight metres long, massive and heavy. It emanated a certain sense of solidity, durability, something that inspired trust. It often gave me support, physically and metaphysically. When I sat at that table I felt strong and safe. I was very attached to it; I had befriended it.

At one time my flat had been filled with hundreds of objects, but they were all stolen. It happened gradually, but the process was merciless. Each time I went on an assignment, my flat grew more spacious; on my return there would be fewer chairs (they were cheap but comfortable) or paintings (admittedly of little value) or clothes (in spite of the damp and mould, in good condition) or pots and pans. Everything disappeared: tables, cupboards, shelves and an Egyptian pouffe (very comfortable). Then the carpets, bedspreads, curtains and hangings went. There was now a space where once there had been the Hoover, the mixer and the fan. What pained me most was the loss of the record-player and records. Music disappeared. Half of my world disappeared. Everything that could be carried under the arm, on the head or the back was stolen. But still they treated me fairly and with kindness. They left me the table, the bed, the kitchen and the fridge. Others, returning from assignments, found they had nothing left, not even nails.

Sometimes, when they were evidently in a hurry, they didn't wait for me to drive far away but burst into the flat as I was leaving, picking up whatever came into their hands. When I returned, I would find Huseini lying on the floor, stifled with a gag.

Huseini was my house boy. The only living being in the flat. There wasn't much to say about him. He would come very early in the morning. I didn't know where he used to come from; he never talked about it. He was small and very skinny, his biceps protruding from under his black skin like little restless knots. I think he had tuberculosis. Not long ago, I also had tuberculosis. I was thin, permanently sweaty with fever.

Huseini walked barefoot; he had short trousers with a hundred patches and a shirt that he had got from me. If he came half-naked, it meant that he had sold his last shirt (or that it had been stolen),

15

Ryszard Kapuściński

and I would have to give him another one. It happened frequently. When it rained he came wrapped in a plastic sheet. It seemed to be the most expensive thing he owned. As soon as he arrived, he would climb to the top of the stairs and wait for the sun to rise above the hill called Mengo and then he would wake me up by knocking at the window. I would jump up from the bed and open the door for him. We would greet each other (in broken Swahili). Then he would go into the kitchen and make some tea. The tea was usually bitter because there was no sugar. He would put the cup on the table and without a word retreat into the kitchen.

With this he had exhausted his duties. He could then leave. In fact, he could stop coming altogether as I didn't need him. But I couldn't fire him because he would never get another job and he had a wife and many children to support. The point was that Huseini didn't know that I couldn't possibly throw him out into the street and so he tried to prove at all costs that he was indispensable. Immediately after making tea he would start tidying up. He swept, hoovered, polished the floor, scrubbed the bathroom and the stairs, washed the windows and the doors. He did all these things very noisily.

He wanted me, at all times, to hear how hard he was working. He would defrost the fridge every day. First he opened it and, with a gesture of helplessness, reproach and appeal, he showed me the inside of the fridge. I'd reply with exactly the same gesture—I know it's empty but there is nothing to fill it with.

The only quiet days were when Huseini had an attack of malaria. Then he came weak, flabby, wet with sweat. He lay down in the kitchen and waited to feel better. I gave him aspirin. When I had an attack of malaria he behaved quietly. I got the impression that he was upset. Sometimes, when he had left I noticed a piece of paper discreetly left on the table: '*Bwana Mkubwa, Kwa heshima nakuandikia barua nikiwa mtumi shi wako . . .*' I did not need to read further. These letters, written by a paid scribe, asked for the next, needless to say non-repayable, loan of money.

Huseini often brought various bits of news with him. They were

16

tales of what happened yesterday in his neighbourhood, or of what he noticed on his way to my house. Frequently he told me that he had seen a dead body.

Whose?

He didn't know, he never asked.

Once he arrived dejected. Crushed. He sat down against the wall, stared ahead and fell silent. After many entreaties he finally told me what had happened. Yesterday, the soldiers had killed one of his children. It was a son. He was three, and his name was Obo.

Translated from the Polish by Alicja Kobiernicka

JEREMY HARDING
POLISARIO

The first time I looked for the wall, I couldn't find it. I had heard comparisons with the Great Wall of China, and had assumed that I would be able to see it from fifty miles away, maybe more. I had imagined there would be concrete fortresses all along its length, which was already 600 miles across the Sahara desert. It was said that more of the wall was being built all the time. No one knew how long it would finally be.

The idea was inconceivable: a wall built to protect the territory of Western Sahara that Morocco had occupied since 1975. It was the invention of Morocco's King Hassan: what better way to keep out Polisario's guerrilla army? It was the Hadrian's Wall of North Africa, with 120,000 troops stationed on it. I imagined that it would rise sheer out of the desert.

In the event, it was quite different.

For two nights and a day, we drove south-west across the desert from Algeria. Near the Western Saharan border, we were met by the local Polisario commander, who escorted us the rest of the way to an observation post about three miles from the Moroccan line of defence. We had reached what Polisario called the Semara Sector, named after the section of the wall opposite the occupied town of Es Semara on the other side.

We followed our guide into the gravel bluffs that shielded us from the array of detection systems planted along the wall—ground sensors, radar and infra-red image-intensifiers—and at the top of a promontory, we peered carefully across a small pile of stones. To begin with, it took me several minutes to pick out anything at all through the binoculars. When I did, I saw only a flat, thin, pale band.

At the crest of a hill, there was a base—a wide circle of ground, lighter in colour than the rest of the wall. It bulged like the sac of a spider. Moroccan soldiers appeared twice. They were black dots in the heat.

We were there for an hour, watching. The wall began to look impressive, but its lethargy, the lack of activity anywhere along it, was exasperating.

The next day Polisario brought up two mortar crews to the gravel bluffs, and it was their pounding that finally roused the wall from its inertia. A short but intensive exchange of fire took place. The guerrillas were using 120-millimetre shells. The first few dropped just short of the base. The rest fell one after another on to their target like a deadly drip from a rafter. The Moroccan rounds were comfortably wide of Polisario's positions, for we were only a mile from the wall, too close for the gunners to get an accurate trajectory over the steep gravel hills and down on to the guerrilla mortar crews. But the units on the wall responded with a feverish extravagance. The air filled with a leaden thunder and kept on filling until you thought it would give with a final, rending crash. Then abruptly it stopped.

I waited two or three minutes before scrabbling down the back of the gravel slope towards the Land Rovers. Some of the fighters had begun shouting at us to move faster. Their voices were harsh, but always with a high, amused excitement. Nuruddin, the guide who had accompanied us from the Algerian border, waited as I stumbled over the gravel. His sense of urgency was just discernible under the mask of courtesy. I was frightened: the Moroccans would surely put up a plane to look for our Land Rovers. It didn't happen. Semara Sector remained quiet for the rest of the day.

An hour and a half later we were camped with the fighters in a dry river-bed. The tea smelled good. It had been prepared by one of the men, who transferred it back and forth between a set of shot glasses and an enamel teapot lodged on a bed of coals in the sand. The fighters enjoyed their tea—always the ritual three draughts. The first, they said, should be sweet, like love; the second bitter, like life; and the third soft, like death.

2

Until 1975, the Western Sahara had been a Spanish colony. There were two historical claims to it, those of the neighbouring countries, Morocco and Mauritania. King Hassan and Moroccan nationalists regarded the Western Sahara as part of a hypothetical Greater Morocco, an empire that also included tracts of Algeria, much of Mali and Mauritania itself. Hassan also wanted control of its phosphate deposits, discovered in the 1960s, and estimated at ten billion tons.

Mauritania's motive was simple: it wanted to be protected from Morocco's expansionism.

There was also a third claimant: the population of the Western

22

WESTERN SAHARA

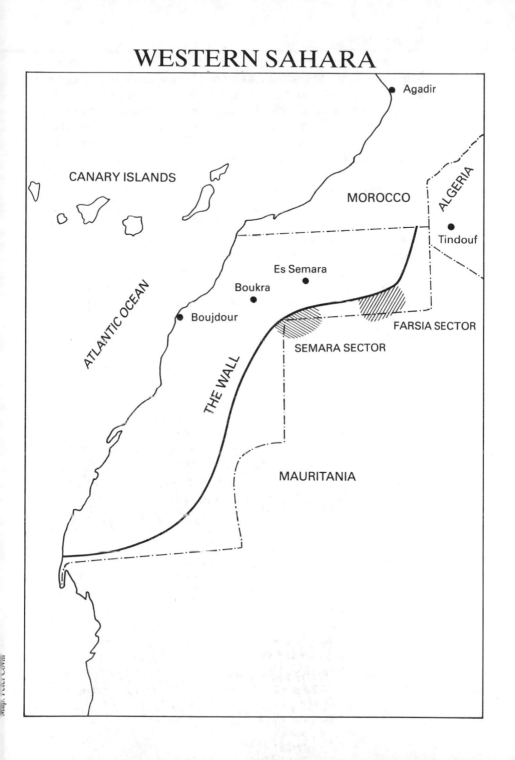

Sahara itself. In the late fifties, that population had rebelled against the Spanish and had been ferociously repressed. In 1973, the Polisario Front was formed, taking its name from the *Frente Popular para la Liberación de Saguia el Hamra y Río de Oro*: the Popular Front for the Liberation of the two provinces of Saguia el Hamra and Rio de Oro, which together made up what was then known as Spanish Sahara.

When Spain prepared to decolonize, Morocco's claims grew more vociferous: Hassan knew that, while Franco was dying, the Spanish would be too preoccupied to make an issue of the desert colony. The United Nations were already pressing Polisario's case when the International Court of Justice at The Hague advised that there was no legal basis on which to enforce Morocco's claim. The Court published its findings in October 1975. Hassan's response was consummate. His Green March mobilized 350,000 Moroccan citizens, who crossed the border under military escort and entered the territory in a well-orchestrated show of popular support for annexation. Moroccan troops were already there.

The Green March forced Spain's hand. Eight days later the Spanish government concluded the Madrid Accords with Morocco and Mauritania, ceding its colony to the two other signatories. The handover was completed in February 1976 and formal partition took place two months later. The inhabitants of what now became known as Western Sahara were simply shuttled from one form of colonial rule to another.

Refugees from the Moroccan occupation began pouring across the borders into Algeria and Mauritania. The Moroccan air force used fragmentation bombs and napalm to hasten their departure. The war had begun in earnest. Polisario declared the birth of its own independent state, the Saharan Arab Democratic Republic, and, backed by Algeria and Libya, set out to harass the two occupying armies. By 1979 Mauritania had been so debilitated by Polisario's guerrilla army that it relinquished its claim and deferred to the movement's legitimacy. Hassan, however, proved more formidable; he had received support from France, the United States and Saudi Arabia.

Even so, Hassan was not going to win an away game in the desert against Polisario; his advisers advocated a change of strategy. If the guerrillas could not be contained, they would have to be excluded. The first section of the huge earthworks devised to keep Polisario from the towns and phosphate mines of Western Sahara was begun in 1980 and finished in the following year. It threw a defensive shield below the town of Es Semara. This was extended a few months later to the phosphate deposits at Boukra and, in 1982, south-west to Boujdour. By 1986 five large sections had been completed; the wall was already over 600 miles long. Polisario could not bring the building of it to a halt, but that day in Semara Sector the guerrillas told me it could be breached or crossed at will. I said I was sceptical, and Nuruddin asked if I took him for an idiot.

The wall was not precisely a wall. It consisted of two sand-and-rubble parapets, three to four metres high, one behind the other. These were separated by an alley where mobile artillery and armoured personnel carriers could be deployed. Every twenty miles or so was a base, between the bases a series of alarm-points, each with roughly forty men. On the other side of the wall there were larger bases with still more troops. The radar and the sophisticated surveillance equipment were said to be sited on the wall itself, with the ground sensors in front. In some sections there was a barbed wire terrace and a random scattering of plastic land-mines.

Nuruddin, who spoke several European languages, often used a French word, *la pourriture*, to introduce his most damning thesis about the wall. 'If we left it alone,' he used to say, 'if we never went near it, the wall would crumble. It is made from desert and it will return to desert. Every hour it is being swept away.' The word in English, I suggested, was decay. Nuruddin said he preferred the French.

A crucial aspect of this *pourriture* was cost. Moving food and water long distances to the soldiers on the wall, repairing radar jammed or broken by sandstorms, constructing new sections and maintaining others—this was an expensive business. In 1983 the US Arms and Disarmament Agency had costed Morocco's occupation of Western Sahara at over three million dollars a day. By 1985 Morocco's external debt stood at thirteen billion dollars. For the entire kingdom, and above all for the throne itself, the wall was a folly. Polisario knew it could not last for ever.

None the less, the wall had forced the guerrillas into a

25

conventional posture. Its slovenly aspect, its reluctance to stir from its torpor, was deceptive. The wall was always active in setting the terms of the conflict; it had kept Polisario out of the most useful land and reduced the value of its greatest assets as a fighting force: speed, daring and a knowledge of the terrain. The great success of the wall, it struck me, was to assert its presence to such an extent that you seldom felt unseen or unaccounted for. It had imposed its own order on the desert by turning vast, homogeneous tracts of rubble into an arcane grid of concourses and pathways, some brightly lit and therefore dangerous, the others dark and apparently safe. Even when you were concealed behind the bluffs in Semara Sector, you still felt vulnerable.

3

Later, in London, sorting through my photographs, I still felt that disturbing sense of exposure. The conflict was more than the war of attrition Polisario had always presented it as being; the wall had made it a war of observation too. The wall waited and watched for Polisario; Polisario watched the wall. I did not know which side's scrutiny would prove the stronger. But it was obvious that the guerrillas had to see without being seen. For Polisario, invisibility was paramount.

Another thing I had learned was that Morocco, like many states in similar circumstances, felt obliged to deny the war's existence. After I returned, there was a conference in Oxford about the Western Sahara. I drove up with my wife, two other journalists and a young German architect, who had moved into our house the day before I'd left for North Africa. He had stayed. My wife was going to show him around Oxford.

It was common at these affairs for a Moroccan contingent to show up from the embassy. That weekend there were several Moroccans, including Belal, a journalist of sorts and an accomplished public relations man attached to the embassy. After a paper touching on the military situation in the territory, Belal stood up. He could not possibly understand, he said, so many references to a war in Western Sahara. What was this talk? True, there had been sporadic trouble years before, involving a handful of disreputable Algerian mercenaries, but that had all been cleared up. Were there not miseries enough in this sorry world without inventing more? The great fortification built by Morocco had surrounded the territory and there were no more mercenaries left to fight.

The audience laughed. It was the laughter of astonishment and it filled the room. Belal stood with a quizzical expression, his head angled sideways so that the wiry hair above his neck crowded against the collar of his leather jacket. Then he sat down, muttering to himself. I had joined in the laughter, but a drab sense of defeat came over me as soon as Belal was back in his seat. Outside, the light was failing, and a March evening had begun to take shape, black and comforting, at the window of the conference room.

Most of what I knew about the wall derived from clippings, statistics, broadcast reports and information from the guerrillas, but after Belal's speech I started to conceive of it differently. At home, the question of the German remained. My wife had fallen in love with him.

I spent hours reading about the wall, ordering my notes and, night after night, poring over my photographs on the kitchen table.

I also listened out for the value of the Deutschmark on the World Service financial reports, hoping this might provide some clue about the survival of my marriage. It was hovering at 188 pfennigs to the dollar. The German, a thoughtful man with a blond moustache, was clearly holding his ground. During his stay, he received packages of sweets and chocolates by post from his mother. These were always too big for the letter-box, a characteristic which somehow made them intolerable. By chewing my way through this horrible confectionery late at night, I must have hoped to come to terms with the demoralizing abundance of the German's life—his elevations and cross-sections, his exemplary mother, his girl-friend in Germany who telephoned daily; and now, to round it off, this piece of good fortune which had befallen him in London. My stoical assault on the chocolates changed nothing.

There was one photograph in particular, which showed a plume of smoke rising from the base where a guerrilla shell had landed. It was poor and uninformative, but it evoked an interest in the wall stronger than any I had felt with Nuruddin and the others.

The last consignment of sweetmeats from Germany reached London in April. I ate my way through most of them, but it was no longer important. My wife had already turned to face a different future. In the meantime, I had grown eager to travel with Polisario again.

4

By the time I returned, the end of 1987, the refugee camps in Algeria had changed. It was a year and a half since I'd seen them. In the interval they had taken on an air of greater stability. Twelve years had elapsed since the Moroccan annexation. Those who survived the exodus had settled in south-west Algeria, near the border, around Tindouf. Gradually they were joined by others, mostly from Mauritania. The Algerians claimed there were 165,000 refugees in four settlements. In a decade these had become orderly places with rudimentary education and health facilities, acres of irrigated garden and a tightly organized social administration.

You could look at these camps, at the mud-brick clinics and schools and the ragged tents in the settlements, without feeling the despair that usually attends the sight of displaced people. Yet the camps were dismally equipped, and the location was a catastrophe, known to be one of the worst stretches of the Sahara: brown gravel, fine sand and little vegetation. Prolonged dust storms produced conjunctivitis among the children and chest complaints among the elderly, who were weakened further by sub-zero temperatures in winter. The older Saharans would never see their land again.

I spent four days in the camps. On the third day, I met several other journalists waiting to visit the front. I would be travelling with Mouloud, who worked for the Algerian Press Service, and Nelson, a sceptical young writer from New York. The simple strategy for his article was to get shot at, courtesy of the US Treasury. 'That's the only way,' Nelson explained, 'to get an American reader interested.' Mouloud, who understood English, simply swivelled his long, unshaven face and stared at the desert.

Polisario claimed they could take journalists across the wall with impunity. We were each hoping to authenticate the claim.

Mouloud was in his early thirties. He said little, ate little and smoked rarely. He wore faded grey trousers which fluttered over his bony legs and a T-shirt which hung straight down from his shoulders. Mouloud had dissent written all over him. It was a bohemian, anti-Islamic dissent, sullen and mercurial. He was a susceptible character; the sight of a beautiful woman in the camps, where the *tchador* was not worn, sent him into a trance.

The night before we left for the front, there was singing and dancing near one of the tents. A young refugee, half Mouloud's age, had taken the floor, moving slowly with her eyes fixed on her outstretched hands, as the women stood in a crescent behind her, clapping and singing. Her beauty was flawless; so much so that it was impossible to watch without some dark sense of regret taking shape as the dance proceeded. I lay back and shut my eyes. Abruptly the musicians doubled the beat; there was a flurry of clapping and loud laughter. I sat up to find Mouloud dancing opposite the girl. At first his gestures were barely visible inside the baggy, motionless clothing. Then he began to fly around her like a length of rope. The Saharan men in the audience stopped clapping and studied this supple outsider encircling the girl as she lowered her eyelids and drew in her stomach.

One of the cadres sitting next to me leaned across and replied to a question from an elder; I heard him explaining that Mouloud was Algerian and watched the elder nod with an air of unease. Mouloud removed his turban, whipped it over the top of the young woman's head, let it drop to her hips and began to draw her towards him. A provocative smile appeared on his face. Three Saharan women emerged from the crowd and started to dance. A group of men followed. The tension was broken and the audience, courteous to the end, was palpably relieved. The next morning, sulky and abstracted, Mouloud was headed for Polisario's war of liberation.

5

Farsia Sector was in the north-east of Western Sahara, about four hours' drive from the refugee camps, another great plain of rubble stretching as far as the eye could see. It was an extraordinary landscape, like a dark ice-rink that had begun to break up.

A dry wind scorched our faces. Polisario's Land Rovers had no windshields; reflective surfaces were a give-away in the desert. There were three Saharans with us in the vehicle: a driver, a cook, and Bashir, a senior official whom I'd met the year before who acted as our guide.

Bashir wore his responsibilities with patience and good humour, and with a *gravitas* which distinguished him from his comrades in Polisario. Their leftism consisted of two trends: nomadic austerity—the spirit of the beleaguered collective—and a lithe, easy-going internationalism that led them to enjoy a rare box of Havana cigars bestowed by a Latin American delegation, to quote from the *Herald Tribune* or to inquire of the European why things had failed to work out between Mick and Bianca Jagger. Something of the old hippy trail from Tangiers down to Western Sahara—or Spanish Sahara as it then was—must have rubbed off on the young intellectuals exiled in Morocco or the Spanish colonial capital. Their revolution had a discernible flavour of the sixties. A traditionalist by temperament, Bashir shared little of their radical style. The revolution was a large, unfamiliar house in which he had found himself. At first, propriety had discouraged him from investigating every recess. After a time, however, he had begun to explore it room by room, object by object, until he had satisfied himself that he was not dreaming. Even so, a part of him was never quite at home there. It was this that made him such an able diplomat.

At first, the route over the dark rubble was scored with tyre-tracks, but gradually, as we drove on, the tracks thinned out. We kept a steady course south-west for a time and then headed due west. There was no change of aspect; only the wind seemed less harsh. North-west of our position lay the phosphate deposits, but there were other minerals scattered throughout the territory, I knew. Iron ore, nickel, chromium, manganese and possibly uranium. We were careering along over a vast bank vault, like children in Zurich skate-boarding down the Bahnhofstrasse.

Before noon we made our first stop for tea and food. The heat stacked high above the ground, and, after an hour, a brisk wind got up, generating small dust devils which pirouetted along the shale and then collapsed. 'That is how you dance,' Bashir said to Mouloud, pointing at a squall. There was general laughter. Like Mouloud, the dust devils had a reckless quality. They were also dangerous, for they could draw Moroccan fire. Dust meant movement and movement meant guerrilla vehicles. Nelson asked how often the Moroccans fired on the dust devils. 'Often enough,' said Bashir. The desert was a great trickster and there was no doubt whose side the fighters felt it was on.

Mouloud lay back and covered his face with a turban. 'Moroccans,' he snorted, as if the word explained every stupidity on the face of the earth.

When we continued, we found that the air breaking over the bonnet of the Land Rover was cooler and the light less absolute. I had been day-dreaming when Bashir took hold of my elbow and drew my attention to the wall. It hung there about seven miles to the north, a yellow band, finer than the rest of the landscape. It had the two qualities I'd discerned in the photos as I ate my way through the German's chocolates: self-importance and menace.

'We're completely exposed,' said Nelson jovially.

It was an odd feeling. With Nuruddin and the others the year before, I had not seen the wall until we clambered up to the observation point. Now it had simply presented itself like some cryptic blemish on the body of the desert, which a moment earlier had seemed in perfect health. Nelson rested one hand on the dashboard and waited for his opening paragraph. But the wall just lay there.

We travelled for a few minutes, holding the fortification dead-level and due north. The consistency of the rubble had changed. The stone was coarser and the flat ground began to pucker and dilate through a choppy heat haze.

Mouloud seemed unimpressed by the earthworks. The cook, however, picked up his rifle and slung it across his knee. The wall disappeared from view as we slid gently behind a gradient. Slight though it was, the incline threw up adequate cover. The three Saharans in the Land Rover were soon talking animatedly through the turbans wrapped across their mouths and noses. I had the driver in perfect profile. By the wrinkles at the corner of his right eye, I could tell he was smiling.

Jeremy Harding

W e linked up with a second Land Rover before resting
for the night. One of the men in the Land Rover,
Mohamed Kori, was the master of tea, and from now on,
he presided over the complex protocol of its making and drinking.
Mohamed Kori was also a poet, and, after dinner, he entertained us
by composing and reciting in classical Arabic as well as his native
Hassaniya.

The next morning over a breakfast of tea, coffee and bread
baked overnight in the cinders of the fire, Bashir informed us that
we would move up to 'observe the wall'.

Polisario officials had frequently declared the need to
'demystify' the wall. It was not clear what this meant, except that it
was a process of sustaining morale until the cost of Hassan's
occupation reached a critical point. If Hassan pulled the army back,
the officers would revolt; if he kept it under-supplied, the conscripts
would mutiny. In either case, the war effort would collapse. Or so
the theory ran. In the meantime, 'demystification' meant coming to
terms with the wall.

None of the fighters had reason to be encouraged about the
state of the war. Year by year old sections of the wall, and sections
of sections, gave way to newer, more advanced or improved
sections, constructed under the protection of large troop
deployments. The defence began to swell, and the guerrillas were
unable to stop its inexorable push towards the limits of Western
Sahara.

The 'strategy of walls' was a blow for the Saharans. When we
reached our first observation point Bashir explained to me that the
best they had managed was delay—delay and diversion. The
guerrillas could mount operations against a section under
construction, he said, and force it off its logical course. If a new
section—and there were now six major sections—had looked set to
run south-west, for example, the guerrillas could impede the
construction and nudge it west. But the time would come when the
Moroccans ran another section further down.

None the less, Bashir and the others were relaxed and
confident during their lengthy studies of Hassan's defence. The
knowledge that they were able to observe the wall without its
observing them appeared to give the guerrillas a psychological

32

edge. We drove from one incline to another, and at each observation post they scrabbled up on all fours, taking turns to study the wall through an old pair of Russian binoculars and talking incessantly as they did so.

As long as the guerrillas watched and talked, handing the binoculars between them with exaggerated care, the monolithic threat of the wall diminished. In this obstinate structure sprawling across their land they seemed to see options and eventualities, evolutions and weaknesses, all infinitely debatable.

Later—I don't remember what time it was—we spotted the white contrail. We had been driving south, away from the wall, or we would have seen the jet earlier. Now everyone turned to watch the vapour trail rise slowly like a strip of lint being stretched to its limit. It continued to extend in our direction and then curved back, leaving a white loop in the sky which was still intact an hour later, when we stopped to rest.

Bashir said it was a reconnaissance flight. In the bright glare of the day I had forgotten that the sky was a useful place from which to prosecute the war of observation. At night you could see the satellites. Nelson claimed that the US passed on valuable information, culled from routine overflights, to Moroccan intelligence. This was possible. Sometimes I mistook a satellite for a star, but within seconds it would betray itself with a tell-tale wink. Whether the satellite was recording anything of value was incidental. It might or might not be, but you knew it was there.

The next day we continued driving from observation post to observation post, and by dusk we were still on the move. It was not a safe time to be travelling—the air was clear and the evening light seemed to flood through it—and I felt uneasy. We drove the two Land Rovers behind a shallow gradient, where some of the men began praying, their backs to the sun. I took a photograph of Nelson—for his grandchildren, he said—and talked for a while to Bashir. Mouloud, whose skin was badly scorched, leaned against one of the vehicles and gazed towards the south. A third Land Rover was approaching. Moments passed. I watched the dust unwind from behind the vehicle. When I could hear the engine, I turned back to watch the fighters at prayer.

The high-pitched whistle of the shell was interrupted by a

muffled bang, like a large door closing miles away; then the whistle resumed, nearer, louder. There was another bang, angry and splintered. A vigorous spout of brown dirt went up a little behind us, to our left. Eight miles from their target, the Moroccans had acquitted themselves well. One shell, casually delivered at a dust column, and now silence—an improbable silence which seemed to flatten and extend sideways. The further it spread, the more capricious the single round began to seem. We waited, but the silence continued to spread until it was a fine patina. I looked at Nelson. He was smiling. 'Tax dollars,' he said. 'Not many, but they'll do.'

Bashir decided to pull us out. There was some shouting, and soon we were driving towards another rubble shield, just to our east. We turned due south a mile later and flew across the shale with darkness gathering in front of us and a curtain of subdued orange light closing across the horizon where the sun had set.

Bashir had told me the proverb once before. 'To the west is the house of fortune; to the east is the house of fire. You must journey south from time to time. As for the north, it is best forgotten.' To the north lay Morocco, the annexationist. To the south lay a vast, uninterrupted field of shale.

An hour later we set up camp. Bashir told us that it was time we observed a harassing operation. Two Polisario units would engage a base with light fire—automatic rifles and 23-millimetre machine-guns—from separate positions south of the wall. That was all.

We nodded.

The night was cool. The coals writhed and divided beneath the teapot. Mohamed Kori recited two verses. The first glasses were distributed, drained and collected again. By the final glass, Bashir was prodding in the sand with a stick. He was restless.

We drove off for a short distance, stopping at the merest hint of an incline. It was the middle of nowhere. We sat and waited. The shale glowed faintly in the starlight, and I could see the silhouettes of the others once my eyes were used to the dark. I could tell, too, that there was flat ground all around us.

'How far are we from the wall?' asked Nelson.

'A comfortable distance,' said Bashir. 'You will see when it begins.'

It began with some brisk tracer fire from the east—a few bursts and the sky darkened again. Then from the west came some longer volleys from mounted 23-millimetre guns.

The Moroccans fired back, their tracers arcing down on to the Polisario positions. The eastern guerrilla unit opened up a second time and immediately the Moroccans replied. The exchange continued and the rubble seemed to get brighter. To the east the Moroccans had put up a flare. It wafted down slowly, throwing a pool of rosy light in front of the wall. The firing stopped and a second flare went up.

'Too high,' said Bashir. Then a flare rose directly in front of us. He ordered us to lie flat with our faces down. A rim of light began to encompass the rubble until every shard glinted. With it came an intolerable feeling of exposure. We lay still with our faces to the ground, waiting in this nightmare of openness until the light subsided. I could imagine no end to it, and no end to being visible in a conflict where invisibility was everything. Polisario's war had been waged for years beneath the gaze of the distant retina, the brilliant lens, the inquisitive technology up on the wall, beneath the sweep of some alien vision scanning the plain for their presence—and now, tonight, for ours.

I could not believe that the flare had guttered and the firing had stopped, or that we were heading away from the wall. I lay back in the juddering Land Rover and looked up at the sky. The constellations swayed over us in a grand conspiracy of surveillance. A star shot low across the sky and hung a fraction too long.

'No, no,' said Nelson, watching me, 'it's not a flare.' Mohamed Kori chuckled and took hold of my elbow. I laughed as well, but the sense of exposure continued. There was much to be said for the cloistered world of the freshwater mussel.

That night, we slept under a tarpaulin slung between the back of the Land Rover and a gaunt acacia. The bitter cold woke me at five, before the light came up. The cook was blowing life back into the embers of the fire as Mohamed Kori rinsed the teapot. I picked up my blankets and went to sit beside them. The cook grinned as the flames clawed their way up a sprig of dry thorn. I no longer welcomed the idea of daybreak.

But if the conflict had begun to upset me, it was getting to Mouloud too. The sun was already up when he woke. He drank his tea in silence, put down the glass and ordered me to take a photograph of him holding a Kalashnikov. There was something threatening about the request. In my disarray, I felt that a whole new agenda had been sprung on me. When I hesitated, he grabbed one of the weapons in a show of bad temper and sat himself down beyond the shade of the tarpaulin, waiting. The fighters made fun of him as I unpacked my camera and hurried after him. I stared through the lens, spinning Mouloud in and out of focus. He had lost so much weight that he resembled a skeleton buried in a pile of laundry. There was loud jeering from Mohamed Kori and the cook as Mouloud clutched the assault rifle like a baby and gazed up at the camera. He ignored them. Bashir yawned and walked off down the dry river-bed.

As the day grew hotter, the shale around us turned darker, until finally it went black—first the black of charred roast, then a glossier black, like wet tar. By walking in a circle, it was easy to establish that every square inch of the landscape was uniformly black and buffed. Nelson, conducting the same experiment a few yards away, resembled a small insect stranded in pitch.

It was hot now: the kind of heat you can hear. In the shade, the flies buzzed and the teapot rattled on a bed of embers. The cook lay back and covered his face to catch some sleep before we moved on.

The wind was not yet rising to break the steady upward curve of the heat. Mohamed Kori stood up and attended to the packs. Bashir pulled his boots on, and the cook collected the tea things, assisted by Mouloud, who had lapsed into a state of eerie solemnity. Nelson refilled his canteen from the water-drum and doused his face. One by one we boarded the Land Rover.

The Land Rover's wheels spun over the black rubble as the wall ducked and rose behind a long sequence of inclines. I felt less and less confident in my judgements of the wall's military character. Its weaknesses had to be set against the sheer force of its presence; there was no gainsaying the wall's six-year push through the desert. I repeated the word 'pourriture', and the tyres coaxed the same word out of the shale. I recalled Nuruddin: 'Do you take me for an idiot?'

The wall was costing the Moroccans $2,000 a minute. Vast sums of money from Saudi Arabia, prodigious consignments of arms and foreign expertise from France, the United States and

Israel had been deployed against an army of some 12,000 guerrillas with little more than a knowledge of the territory, a fleet of Land Rovers and two Third-World backers, one of which, Libya, had already pulled out. The wall was dangerous, undoubtedly. It was also a magnificent structure of denial—the biggest monument to denial in the whole of Africa—but it was not without a certain pathos. Its capacity to play the adamant father and reduce Polisario to children, sneaking up on it, gazing at it, plotting and whispering—this was a condition of pathos, because in politics there are no enduring fathers.

As we rested in the afternoon, I fell asleep. I dreamed that my wife was in our living-room, hunched beside the German at his drawing-board. I entered. She handed me one of his drawings. 'We've decided to make some alterations,' she explained. 'It's a conversion.' She burst into tears. In the drawing were two figures, a man and woman, making love. The German placed a box of sweets in her hands. She opened it decisively and sorted through the contents. Several empty wrappers dropped to the floor. Next, we were in a park, walking through deep drifts of sweet-wrappers towards a pane of glass in open ground. We stopped; she looked eagerly through the glass and checked her watch. We shook hands. I made my way back across the autumnal carpet of wrappers, rustling under my feet. 'You will give us away,' she called after me, 'if you can't be quieter.'

I woke to find a dozen fighters sitting in the shade. Bashir and Lih El Hadj, the local Polisario commander, who had arrived while I slept. They were putting the finishing touches to a plan to take us across the wall. In due course Bashir looked across at us and smiled. 'Now that you have all rested well, you must prepare to pay the Moroccans a visit this evening. Comb your hair and put on your best clothes in case they invite us for *tagine*.'

6

That was the trick, obviously: to drive at a ninety-degree angle to the wall, head-on. We were within ten miles of it when we set out in two vehicles, one directly behind the other, moving at fifteen miles per hour. In the darkness, they eased over the rubble incline which had shielded us all afternoon and on towards the point where they would show up on any thermal-imager in the sector. At the crest, the drivers cut their speed to about two miles per hour, the engines barely turning over. I felt little, except a desire to get this over with. At the same time, I was confident that the exercise would pass off uneventfully; events, or a lack of them, could always be organized for the benefit of visitors.

Bashir assured us that the barbed wire in front of the wall had been cut months earlier and that Polisario sappers, who worked by hand, had removed the land-mines.

'Terrific,' said Nelson, 'that's settled then. Terrific.'

The vehicles sputtered forward.

Holding your course at ninety degrees to the wall, you were, in theory, at your least visible. This geometric conflict of inclines and angles required extraordinary precision. You had to approach in a straight line. Any deviation, by even a degree or two, would present the Moroccans with an increasingly visible target. But then you could only run at ninety degrees towards one point on the wall, and in doing so, you were approaching other points—an adjacent base, for instance—off the right angle. It was complicated. I consoled myself with the thought that the Saharan drivers and unit commanders had all this down. They were a desert people with a sense of the stars and trigonometry.

We stopped. Bashir climbed down without opening the door, crept to the other vehicle and whispered to the driver. He then returned to our Land Rover and told us that from now on there was to be no talking. The vehicles took up again at a snail's pace. I was tinkering with my tape-recorder when Mouloud pressed my arm, leaned across and whispered my name.

'Yes?' I said.

'Just then,' he said in French, 'I had a feeling very like fear.'

This broke me out of my abstraction and into a curious emotion, akin to envy. I had been feeling quite deadened.

To my consternation, it occurred to me that the guerrillas might be deceiving us. Suppose we were being taken to an abandoned stretch of the wall? Were these ghostly fighters— ghostly because Morocco denied their existence—escorting us to an equally ghostly defence? Later we would report on the vulnerability

38

of Hassan's monument. Polisario would have put their message across that the multi-million-dollar fortification was easily breached; you could slip over it any day of the week.

Mouloud repeated in my ear, 'I had a feeling very like fear,' and added, 'but I'm going anyway.' When he sat back, he could not draw his breath. It lodged somewhere behind his collar-bone and he began to cough. The cough became an extended wheeze and Bashir swung round in admonition.

There was a second group of guerrillas waiting for us near the wall. We followed them through the darkness in single file. For several minutes, my boots ground into the shale until one of the guides fell back, caught me by the wrist and led me over the ground with such skill that I was no longer making a sound. We were moving roughly parallel with the wall, it seemed, towards a point where we could climb on to it at a comfortable distance from any base or alarm-point. The ground was rising slightly now and it was sandier, which suggested another dry river-bed.

After a few minutes, we passed a mysterious well of light about two hundred yards to our right. Later one of the guerrillas said it was a distant flare, but Mohamed Kori insisted that it was a beam from a searchlight. Perhaps. I felt deeply endangered by this light. I no longer envied Mouloud his fear.

We had been moving in a curve, getting nearer the wall, when we were ordered to lie down. I began by sitting half-heartedly. Bashir moved back to ensure that each of us was lying flat.

'What's happening?' I whispered when he reached me.

'We're waiting,' he said. 'Lie down.' It grew cold. About three yards up ahead of me was Mouloud, beyond him Nelson, and beyond Nelson, Mohamed Kori and another fighter. No one moved. The minutes dragged by, and then a thin wailing sound began up ahead.

It was a despondent, animal sound, which rose to an intolerable pitch and then stopped. A few seconds later it began again, much louder. Both the fighters sat up rigid. In the dark, I could just make out Mouloud's legs beating quietly on the sand.

It seemed to be an asthma attack, and it threatened to alert the Moroccans. By the time Mouloud began to wail again, Bashir and Mohamed Kori were crawling down the file to attend to him.

39

Mouloud struggled to check the attack. It turned first into a wheeze, then into a series of staccato gasps and then back once again to a wheeze. When they reached Mouloud, the two men squatted down beside him, one with his hands on his forehead and the other wrapping his arms around his chest. They placed his face in a turban and one of them hit him hard on the back, while the other whispered into his ear. There was a terse gurgling noise and then Mouloud began breathing regularly again. He gave out a very low chuckle, insolent and difficult, and rolled on to his side. Bashir and Mohamed Kori slid away to the front of the file and lay on their stomachs.

Ten minutes later Bashir crept back down. 'Listen carefully,' he whispered, 'and you will hear Moroccan voices coming from the base.'

'Where is the base?' I asked.

'One hundred and fifty metres,' he said and pointed west.

I could see an outline; perhaps it was a base perimeter. It was safer to be close to a base than an alarm-point: the base perimeters were big and doubtless poorly patrolled. I listened intently. I could hear something or other, but I wasn't sure what. 'I can't hear them,' I said, and Bashir went to check on Mouloud.

It was another fifteen minutes before we climbed the wall. We edged along the sand for a few hundred yards and then it was there, taking us by surprise again.

Like a child in a dark garden startled by the sight of a sheet on a clothes line, I felt my heart racing. Pale and wrinkled, suspended in the darkness, the rampart even looked like drying linen. In a few moments I was over the first parapet and walking gingerly along a set of tank tracks. I wondered how old they were. When Nelson and Mouloud had cleared the first parapet, we climbed slowly on to the second. We were now in occupied Western Sahara.

We sat there in the uncompromising stillness of the desert. Then, unaccountably, we heard stones pattering down to the base of the wall. Bashir leaned across and muttered in my ear, '*La pourriture.*' We climbed down the second parapet and he produced a strip of green rag from his pocket. He knelt, scooped up a handful of sand, wrapped it in the rag and presented it to me. It was for the Polisario delegate in London. 'With greetings,' he whispered, 'from Bashir Ahmed.'

John Ryle
The Road to Abyei

John Ryle

Kalash au bilash; Kalash begib al kash
(You're trash without a Kalashnikov;
get some cash with a Kalashnikov)

Catch-phrase in Darfur

Mark drove me back from the party on Street Thirty-one in his new Land Rover. We took a wrong turning on Sharia el Nil, the road that runs along the Blue Nile behind the Presidential Palace, and found ourselves driving down an unlit street near the United Nations building, when we just missed running over the leg of a man sleeping in the roadway. There were two or three dozen bodies lying half on and half off the sidewalk, long-limbed, dark-skinned, wrapped in blankets against the cold. They were Dinkas from the South, street-hawkers, hungry and homeless. Each of them had a cardboard suitcase full of cigarettes for sale—red and white Bringi or Behsons in gold packets, the high-tar version they sell in the Sudan. During the day they plied their trade in the arcades between the Acropole, the relief workers' hotel, and the old Excelsior. At night they dodged the police patrols, snatching sleep between alarms, eyes half open, watchful, like a herd of antelope.

Mark and I were working for one of the myriad relief agencies that had come to the assistance of southerners displaced by the five-year civil war. I had just arrived in the Sudan to report for the agency's London office on their operations in Khartoum and points south. Mark was a field officer in the far west, on the front line of the famine. We were spending a week in Khartoum, where half a million or more of the displaced lived in camps and shanty towns. Then we were heading for Abyei, a government-controlled Dinka town on the border with the South, six days' journey by land in the dry season, 500 miles by air.

In early 1988, 20,000 southerners had sought refuge in Abyei—four times the normal population of the town. In May that year the first report from Abyei appeared in the western press. It was by Carol Berger, a Canadian journalist I first met in the early eighties, when I was doing field-work in Dinkaland and she was a freelance in Khartoum. 'Abyei's muddy streets,' she wrote,

> are crowded with people near death. Women, children, teenage boys and the elderly—many no more than skeletons—have taken refuge in a virtual Auschwitz . . . But more appalling still is the backdrop to the death scene—Arab merchants and their strong sons carrying out business as usual . . . For the past two years, Dinka men found among the town's destitute have been killed as collaborators or suspected rebels. Their throats are cut and their bodies dumped outside the town.

The article described the occupation of Dinka grazing lands and the theft of their cattle by local Misseriya Arabs. 'For the length of our journey,' it concluded, 'ragged bands of Dinka passed . . . being taken to work on Misseriya farms as slave labour.'

Behind the militias was a Khartoum government bent on Islamicizing the country; on the other side in the war was a southern Sudanese guerrilla army extending its control of the South from bases on the Ethiopian border. The strategy of the National Army: arm the militias to loot and burn southern villages, steal their cattle and drive their inhabitants into the North.

John Ryle

The next morning I walked out of the Acropole into the brightness and noise of downtown Khartoum and spoke to one of the cigarette salesmen. His name was Elia Makuac; he was twenty years old and came from Bor, in the southern part of Dinkaland, where the civil war had started five years earlier. He had not been driven out by Arabs, but by militiamen from another southern tribe. (There are many tribes in the South; many militias.) Half of Makuac's family died on the journey north. Bor is a long way from Khartoum—more than 700 miles. There were other hostile groups on the way and precious little food.

I had not been in Khartoum since the war began. In the old days you wouldn't have seen Dinkas like Makuac, with his splayed teeth and candelabra-shaped head scar. In those days you didn't see many people from the South at all: there were Nuer construction crews on the high steel of the half-built office-blocks and cabals of educated Dinka at the bar of the Hotel Excelsior; otherwise the migrants from the South were lost in the northern throng. Ten years on, the Excelsior was closed and liquor was banned but the presence of southerners in Khartoum was overwhelming.

It was the main change. The fabric of the city remained the same: dust parks and cemeteries, half-buried plastic bags glinting underfoot, houses of mud and mouldering concrete, pot-holes, battered taxis, sleek ministerial Mercedes—the usual Third World road show. But now—it startled me—the streets were full of southerners, refugees from the periphery, come to haunt the capital, the centre of Arab hegemony. They were mostly Nilotic tribespeople from the great savannah—Dinka, Nuer, Shilluk—jet-black and tall as trees. In parts of Khartoum there were so many it was like being in a southern town.

Scorning the *jallabia* and preferring western clothes, the southerners looked defiant, as though they owned the place. But they owned nothing. The vast majority of them were destitute, living on the street, or in *bidonvilles* on the periphery, where the city meets the sand, in houses made of cardboard and tin. They lived on rubbish tips, in the industrial zone, between mountains of toxic

NORTH-EAST AFRICA

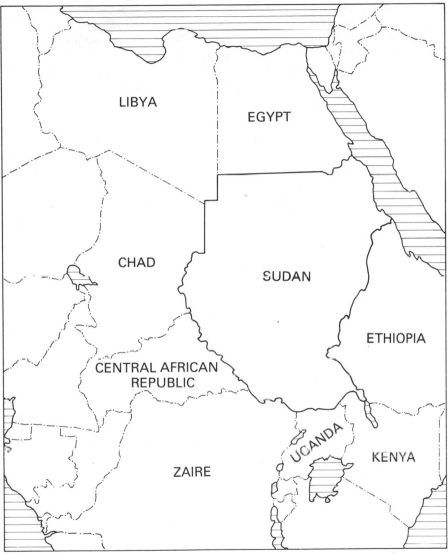

LIBYA

EGYPT

CHAD

SUDAN

ETHIOPIA

CENTRAL AFRICAN
REPUBLIC

UGANDA

KENYA

ZAIRE

Map: Peter Covill

waste. There was no firewood to be had; no work; they had to pay for water, so they could not afford to wash. Winter was coming and they were cold at night. These were people from the warm South, a land that had once flowed with milk and honey.

Milk and honey, but not much else. As far as modernity goes the South has nothing. It is the victim of underdevelopment, or the beneficiary, depending on your point of view. There are a few hundred miles of malfunctioning railway, five or six hospitals, about a hundred yards of paved road, barely any commercial agriculture. But there is land; and there are rivers; and the subsistence economy of southern peoples—agricultural, pastoral and piscatorial—offers them a kind of wealth. In the case of Nilotes this wealth takes the form of cattle, huge auroch-like beasts, the great-horned descendants of the extinct wild cattle of the Nile valley, interbred with lateral-horned zebu imported from Asia in ancient times. The Nilotic peoples, chiefly the Dinka and their southern neighbours, the Nuer, possess very large herds of these cattle, or did, before the war. In Khartoum the displaced Nilotes had no land, no cattle; they did not even have goats. The only livestock to be seen were on their way to the slaughter house. And they did not belong to them, not any more.

T he famine in Abyei was not the only disaster story from the Sudan that summer. Floods washed away the shanty towns in Khartoum; displaced southerners were shown living in seas of excrement from flooded pit-latrines. From the besieged cities of the South came photographs of marasmic four-year-olds with stick limbs and oversize heads, looking like extraterrestrial beings. Hundreds of thousands of southerners were fleeing northwards. There were stories of men, women and children killed, tortured or taken into slavery on the way. The South, it seemed, was a charnel-house. The Dinka, in particular, some of these stories claimed, were facing extinction.

The last claim was hard to believe. Smaller ethnic groups in the borderlands between North and South had indeed been decimated and driven from their territory. The Dinka, however, are not a small tribe; they are a large and dynamic people, the largest in the region, celebrated in the texts of social anthropology. There are—or were before the war—more than a million Dinkas, maybe two million. Their territory is a thousand miles across. Despite the Dinkas' pastoral mode of life they cannot be considered an archaic remnant like the Masai of Kenya. They form a politically active ethnic bloc with highly articulate spokesmen in Khartoum and the outside world.

The first Dinka I ever met was from Abyei, when I was a graduate student at Oxford. Francis Mading Deng was the author of a number of books about his people and about to become his country's ambassador to the Scandinavian countries. I had written a paper on the ethnology of the Nile Basin and called to see my supervisor, as usual, at a pub in Oxford. I found him with three Sudanese visitors. My supervisor was showing them a sketch-map I had included in my paper to show the distribution of southern tribes. I was introduced to the Commissioner of Upper Nile Province, to a notable from the same area, then to Francis. He shook my hand and pointed at the map, at an area just beyond the border of the southern region. The shading I had assigned to the Dinka tribes nudged that of the Misseriya, the Arab cattle-keeping people to the north. 'I think,' said Francis, 'you have given some Dinka territory to our Arab brothers.'

'And,' said the Commissioner, 'you seem to have put my own village in Ethiopia.'

It was particularly unfortunate that the part of Dinkaland I had annexed to the Misseriya was Francis's home, the town and district of Abyei. I had an excuse, however: as I understood it, Dinkas were inhabitants of the southern Sudan, the non-Muslim part of the country—the pagan bit, as it was sometimes flippantly referred to. Abyei was in the North, so I had assumed it was in the territory of a northern tribe.

In fact Abyei was also in the province of Kordofan, and the

whole of the south-western corner of the province was the territory of the Ngok, one of the Dinka tribes. At independence the Paramount Chief of the Ngok—Francis's father—had judged that the future of his people would be better served by remaining in the North, closer to the power centre of the country. Not all the Ngok notables agreed with him. Throughout the seventies there was talk of a referendum to resolve the anomaly of Abyei, but the political state of the country was not amenable to such adjustments.

Ten years on, my cartographic error did not look so innocent. It seemed that the Arab Misseriya inhabitants of Kordofan were bent on following the logic of the boundary. Abyei was under military occupation, most of the Ngok had been displaced from their villages and the Misseriya militias moved freely through their land.

The next day I visited Hillat Kusha, a huge shanty town in Khartoum North where the least fortunate southerners ended up. I went there with Majak, a Dinka historian I had asked to accompany Mark and me to Abyei. Majak specialized in relations between the Nilotic peoples, of which the Dinka are the largest, and Baggara Arab tribes like the Misseriya with whom they share grazing grounds. He was from Abyei himself. And he knew about shanty towns: he lived in one.

To get to Hillat Kusha we followed the railway north to the city limits. There, in an ash-grey wasteland where dust and smoke swirled in the wind, were two separate settlements, Combo and Hillat Kusha proper. Hillat Kusha means 'the place of garbage'. Twisted metal, broken glass and human faeces littered the black sand. Women picked through the refuse in search of scraps. Somehow amid the squalor they managed to have clean clothes. But the reek of home-brewed *merissa* and distilled *aragi* hung over the settlement. The raised voices of drunken elders could be heard in the shade.

The Dinka chief at Hillat Kusha was sober, but he'd had enough of outsiders' inquiries. Why all these questionnaires? he demanded of Majak. Always questions and no blankets. Why do they send you big fish to eat us little ones? And what is happening to this information? What is the government doing with it? Why all this talk about Dinkas? Why are they victimizing us?

Majak explained that we were not the government, that the agency we worked for had been helping the displaced elsewhere and was trying to find the best way to help people here. But we both knew the chief had a point. In Hillat Kusha they had seen more relief workers than they had seen relief. They had seen journalists and television crews, but they had never seen themselves in a newspaper or on TV.

What was happening to the information?

I couldn't say. I still can't.

I spoke to a Dinka from the southern town where I had lived in the early eighties. I recognized the name of the chief in his village. I asked him the names of some of the Dinka tribal sections in the area, names that I had forgotten and was trying to recollect, but he could remember fewer of them than I could. Distance and *merissa* were eating up his memory.

That was one reason for collecting information here in the diaspora: old-fangled salvage anthropology. It's a promise anthropologists have often made: 'We are asking these questions so we can write down the history of your people for your children and your children's children.' Generations of anthropologists have said this sort of thing and meant it quite sincerely because they fall in love in the plural, not with persons but peoples, and so they have an interest in their survival. But it rang a little hollow on the rubbish tips of Khartoum. No one knew what would become of the children born in this place. It was unlikely that any of them would ever learn to read.

John Ryle

That night we drove back along the airport road by the line of social clubs that service the local professional and trading élites: the Army Club, the Armenian Club, the Greek Club, the Arab Club. Here expatriate workers mix with Sudanese, those few middle-class Sudanese who are managing to sustain their standard of living amid the wreckage of the national economy. From a tent in the garden of one of the clubs came the sound of music playing. It was 'Rivers of Babylon', the Melodions' reggae setting of Psalm 137. The words of the psalmist of Israel wafted towards the new mosque by Suq Two as the moon rose over the airport.

> *By the Rivers of Babylon*
> *Where I sat down,*
> *Yea and I wept*
> *When I remembered Zion.*

Drought, floods, locusts. War, famine, pestilence. The pale horse of death. It did seem, with the current diaspora of southern peoples, that the disaster in the South was of biblical proportions.

While I was in Khartoum, there was a flurry of peace talks between the government and the rebels. Abolition of the *shari'a* laws was the rebels' first demand; but the government, with military backing from Libya and Iraq, showed no signs of retreat from Islamicization. There was much talk of a cease fire and a constitutional conference. Meanwhile fighting continued in the South and refugees continued to come. It was the fifth year of the war. Among men of good will in North and South there was an air of desperation. 'Peace,' said a headline in a Khartoum newspaper, 'is the milk of birds.'

And there was no end in sight to the war. The first civil war in Sudan began in 1956, more or less as soon as the country achieved independence. It ended in 1972; the current one began a decade later. The country is fatally divided. North and South; centre and periphery; Arab and African; Nilotic and non-Nilotic; Muslim and

Photo (preceding pages): Hutchison Library

52

non-Muslim. The first war was fought by southern separatists. But no African war of secession has yet succeeded: Biafra, Katanga, Western Sahara, Eritrea stand as warnings to secessionists. If such wars worked the face of the continent would be different: north-east Africa, certainly, would be comprehensively balkanized; a giant country like Sudan, the biggest in Africa, would cease to exist.

In 1972, after seventeen years of war in the Sudan the separatists settled for regional autonomy. There was ten years of peace, more or less, and increasingly dictatorial government. In the early eighties, with southern autonomy eroded, the country half-bankrupt, an oil strike in the South and Islamic law imposed in the North, southerners had taken up arms again. This time the stakes were higher: the rebels' programme involved transforming the political economy of the whole Sudan, redirecting development to areas outside the central zone. This would end, they said, the hegemony of the Khartoum élite, composed of the members of a few Arab families—politicians, army officers, commission men and leaders of religious brotherhoods—the same élite that had, directly or indirectly, controlled the country since independence.

The rebel forces, calling themselves—inevitably—the Sudan People's Liberation Army, were led by a Dinka, Dr John Garang de Mabior, a former Colonel in the National Army with a doctorate from Iowa State. By 1988 the SPLA controlled the greater part of the rural South. The government held the bigger towns, by a thread.

Maps of the Past

I visited the Survey Office, the old house of maps, an oasis of charm and efficiency in the midst of bureaucratic decay. There were women in high-heeled sandals, with gold ear-rings and *taubs* that fluttered beneath the ceiling fans, wafting sandalwood across the counter. For five Sudanese pounds, less than a dollar on the currency black market, they would sell you 4,000 square miles of desert or delta, swamp or savannah on a 1:250,000 sheet, rolled into a tube wrapped up in an old copy of *Al Usbu* or *Al Ayyam*. Their fingertips were tawny with henna, their nails painted silver, like pools in a desert. At their command male clerks scaled great wooden edifices composed of metre-square pigeon holes stuffed with bales of maps, in search of whichever you wanted of the 150-odd sheets it takes to cover the huge expanse of the Sudan.

Most of these maps remain unchanged since the country was first surveyed in the 1930s. And that is how it should be, because, despite civil wars and political upheavals, hardly anything in these places has changed since then. 'Sacred baobab tree', they say. 'Many cattle camps'; 'Major Titherington followed this route in 1931'; 'Open grassy plain'; 'Unsurveyed'. Some of the sheets, those covering the Libyan desert, are great blanks; others are dense with rivers, footpaths and human settlements. They bear the names of southern places: Malakal, Kurmuk, Wau, Nyamlell, Abyei. Once these names had made me quick with longing for the South. Now the shadow of death lay over them.

I gazed at the map of Abyei, covering the area up to Aweil, between the river that the Dinkas call Kir and that the Arabs call Bahr-el-Arab, southwards to the River Lol. The North-South border zig-zagged across the swamps and grazing lands between the two rivers.

It was more than a decade since I had made my cartographic error in Oxford. Since then I had got to know the South at first hand. With my finger I traced the route I had taken to Aweil eight years before. The villages in the area had been the most densely populated in the South, the richest in livestock, their cattle byres heady with smoke and the exhalations of animals. Now the byres and villages were empty, burned to the ground. In Aweil, I remembered, I had lost a dozen games of Hearts to the Police Chief. Where was he now? In the North? In the SPLA? These days you had to make such inquiries, discreetly, about all your southern acquaintances. Behind such inquiries lay the further question: were they alive or dead?

The map of Abyei was a map of the past. And not only for me. The clerk who fetched it watched as I followed the road to Aweil with my finger. I could see he was a southerner. 'Have you been there?' he asked in English. 'That is my village. People are suffering, dying there. Many people come. They come here now. Suffering, suffering.' He told me he had sixteen relatives staying in his two-room house, most of them living on his meagre salary, about forty dollars a month. In Khartoum, where every southerner with a home or an income has a dozen dependents, the kinship system is at breaking point. Sooner or later some of those relatives would have to move out. And they would have nowhere to go but the shanty towns. Suffering, suffering.

On my last day in Khartoum I visited the sister of Robert Maker, a Dinka who had been my research assistant eight years before. She was a doctor, working for the Sudan Council of Churches. Robert had been a student in Alexandria, home on vacation when we worked together. In 1985 I heard that Robert had joined the SPLA, and, in 1988, in May, that he had been killed in action at Bentiu, site of Sudan's first oil well, the optimistically named Unity I.

In her makeshift office his sister and I discussed the problem of looking after the huge numbers of the malnourished and sick in the shanty towns where she worked. We talked about the news from the South, about the current peace negotiations, about her brother's death. I gave her a copy of the book he helped me write.

I remembered the day seven years before when Robert Maker and I bicycled to Karic, his home village, in the territory of the Duor, a Dinka section that had been involved in a year-long tribal feud with their neighbours. The feud had left twenty-eight dead. It seemed shocking to me at the time. Twenty-eight dead! How many were dying now as a result of the war?

A week or two before, Robert and I had taken one of the victims of the feud to the hospital with a spear through his thigh. There was a drunken orderly at the hospital.

'Fucken Dinkas,' he said, 'fucken Dinkas. He is just a fucken

Dinkas—always fighting—never stop. Fight, fight, fight.'

'Only when provoked,' said Robert, with a smile that could have been mistaken for gentleness.

'And that is always,' said the orderly.

Robert smiled and smiled. 'We are not fighting now,' he said. The youth with a spear through his thigh got treated and recovered. Not Robert. Guns made it a lot easier to get killed. They upset the balance of violence.

Driving westwards, All Souls'Day

On the first day of November the three of us left Khartoum—Mark, Majak and I. Driving south out of the city I felt only elation: road fever, relief at leaving, joy at the prospect of seeing village Africa again, the Africa that endures despite famine, civil war and economic collapse. As we drove out of the city we dodged road-blocks and spirals of black smoke from truck tyres set on fire by rioters. They were protesting against the food shortages. There was no sugar on the open market in Khartoum; no milk; no milk powder; and often no bread. Only anger in the market place. It seemed like a good time to be leaving.

At the edge of the urban area was a tent city established for victims of the floods. Then came the desert: some scrubby grass left over from the rains, a few fields of stunted dura, spiky thorn bushes, no trees, no shade. The road from Khartoum runs parallel to the Nile, but you wouldn't know it. There are no tributaries for 600 miles. Grey was the colour, the colour of stones. A German construction engineer was supervising the resurfacing of the road. As we drove past I saw one of the labourers kneeling to say his morning prayers on the virgin blacktop as though it was a prayer-mat newly unrolled.

We drove all day through the desert. There was a week's journey ahead of us, but every mile brought us closer to the grasslands, closer to the West, and—for Majak—closer to home.

Opposite: Khartoum

We reached the bridge at Kosti at dusk. Here, where the road and the railway meet the river, we saw water for the first time. The river was half-choked with water hyacinth, a floating plant with gaudy purple flowers that has blocked many of the great waterways of Africa. Kosti was full of Dinkas who had come from the places we were going to.

The hardtop ended in Kosti. Night fell. We left the river and headed west. Dust swirled in our headlights. Mark had learned a lesson from the *suq* truck drivers—he liked to drive after dark, when the night kept the engine cool. I could hear him trying to raise Khartoum on the radio—'Do you read me? Do you read me?'—as I dozed on the kapok mattresses in the back of the pick-up.

Two months earlier, Mark had been in El Meiram, a small town near the Bahr-el-Arab, about fifty miles west of Abyei. Reports had begun to come through of another influx of southerners, along the railway that runs from Aweil, a Dinka area, into Southern Kordofan. They did not come by train—there had only been one train the whole year—they walked, and were congregating at a railway station in the territory of the Misseriya, whose militia had been responsible for the raiding in Abyei district.

In September, towards the end of the rains, Mark set off for El Meiram with an Oxfam water engineer. Their Land Rover got stuck in the mud and they walked the last eighteen miles to the police post in a tropical rainstorm. There they found a two-man medical team from Médecins Sans Frontières and about 5,000 Dinkas. The Dinkas were naked, emaciated, without shelter or possessions and dying at the rate of fifty a day. Unburied bodies lay on the ground, covered in flies; vultures pecked at them; there were no tools to dig graves; some of the corpses had been dismembered by hyenas in the night. A Unicef team responsible for supplementary feeding of malnourished children had given up and left when the rains set in three months before. Nearly all the young children had died. The two French doctors were the Dinkas' only source of help. The doctors were themselves in an advanced stage of exhaustion. After two days at El Meiram, Mark set off back north. I remember reading his report in England. The mortality rates at El Meiram had been some of the highest in the world, several times higher than at Korem in 1984, when the BBC broke the news of the Ethiopian famine. Mark said it was the worst thing he had ever seen.

Mark was in his twenties, a theology graduate and a veteran of disasters. It doesn't take long to become a veteran in the relief business. Until recently he had been working in Somalia; he had run a refugee camp on the Chadian border during the last great catastrophe in the Sudan, the Darfur famine of 1984–85. Mark liked the Sudanese he worked with, and the racial antagonism that persisted in many cases between northerners and southerners bothered him.

Where he worked this antagonism was hard to forget. His base was in Ed Da'ein, one of the towns we were to visit on our way to Abyei. Ed Da'ein was a railway town in Southern Darfur and tribal centre of the Rezeigat, Arab cattle-keepers whose territory borders that of the Dinkas of Aweil.

In 1987 Ed Da'ein had been the scene of a massacre of hundreds of defenceless Dinka migrants, men, women and children, shot or hacked to death in the streets of the town, or burned alive in boxcars in the railway station while the local police absented themselves. There had been no official investigation of the massacre and no charges brought, although survivors still living in the town were able to identify dozens of the perpetrators. The facts were only public knowledge thanks to the efforts of two northern intellectuals, teachers from Khartoum who, on their own initiative, wrote and published a report on the events. One of them was imprisoned and interrogated for his pains.

The spectre of such ethnic conflict haunted relief workers. Although only two of the Dinka settlements were in Rizeigat territory, the events in Ed Da'ein, it was becoming clear, were part of a wider pattern of violence involving repeated raids by Rizeigat militia in the Aweil area, where the great majority of Dinka migrants came from. Aweil had been the most densely populated area of the South, and the militias had seemingly been given *carte blanche* by government authorities to loot and burn. Hundreds of thousands of cattle had been stolen. Cattle are the pastoralist's famine reserve: if the harvest fails there is milk and meat, or a cow can be sold for grain. When the militias burned their crops, the Dinka villagers had nothing to fall back on. On top of that came the demands of the SPLA: rebel units might demand anything they had. There was no food in southern towns. In Aweil, a hundred miles south-west of Abyei, there were rumours of mass starvation and epidemic disease. Here, as in other parts of Africa, the equation is simple and cruel: war plus drought equals famine. So the Dinkas were driven inexorably northwards.

We drove late that night and all the next day. The road to the western Sudan is not always a road. Sometimes it is a river-bed; sometimes it is the railway; sometimes it narrows to deep ruts that snag the transmission; sometimes it divides and re-divides into a maze of tracks, like a river delta. In the rainy season such a road may well become a river. There are long stretches of black cotton soil, viscid self-mulching clay that has wheels spinning helplessly, digging in deeper and deeper. Tough. This is the high road to the hunger zone. During the Darfur famine of 1984–85 trucks struggled for weeks to reach the West along this road. We were fortunate; it was the dry season and we had a new vehicle. It only took us twenty-four hours to drive the 250 miles from Kosti to our next destination, El Obeid, the capital of Kordofan.

SUDAN

Nile

Port Sudan ●

Northern
Darfur

Omdurman
●
Northern
Kordofan

Khartoum

El Obeid
●

Blue Nile

White Nile

Southern
Darfur

Southern
Kordofan

Abyei
●

Malakal
●

Bahr-el-Ghazal

El Buheyrat

Jonglei

John Ryle

A Wicked Business

We spent a day in El Obeid with Kuol Deng Majok, Paramount Chief of the Ngok Dinka, a kinsman of Majak. We found him in his rented house near the railway line, the line that led back to Kosti and the North, a route that many of his people had followed in their flight from Abyei. Chief Kuol was a young man who spoke some English; he, too, had been displaced. He was waiting in El Obeid for a chance to return to Abyei.

The Ngok, he explained, were on the front line of the conflict between Arab and Dinka tribes; they were the first to be affected by the war. Although the leadership of the tribe dissociated itself from the rebels, this availed them nothing. Misseriya Arabs with automatic weapons looted freely in the Abyei area in 1984 and 1985, stealing cattle and abducting women and children. It was a return, said chief Kuol, to the last years of the nineteenth century, when Arabs had raided the Dinka for slaves.

On Christmas Eve in 1986, an Arab raiding party appeared on the outskirts of Abyei with stolen cattle and prisoners, men, women and children, openly tied together with ropes. The police did nothing; the army did nothing: it seemed they got their share of the spoils. The attitude of the authorities in Abyei, who were Arabs, was that the villages affected by the raids were supporting the SPLA: the abducted Dinkas were not slaves but hostages. Chief Kuol himself was smuggled out of the town. Since he left there had been a continual stream of Ngok people through El Obeid, leaving Abyei for the North, but no government action against the militias. Chief Kuol reckoned that by now the majority of his people had, like him, left their home territory.

The migration of the Ngok after 1986 was matched by an influx of other Dinka tribes into Abyei. The militias raided villages further south, where people had no previous contact with them. People in these villages did not leave their homes until they were reduced to starvation. Arriving in Abyei they found an unfriendly administration in league with the militiamen. Traders were charging hundreds of pounds for a sack of dura. The roads were closed because of the rains. These were the southerners—fifteen or twenty thousand of them—who had finally made the headlines, after several thousand had died. And after these, there would be more: for every one who left Abyei there was another to take his place.

We left El Obeid the following day. In the small towns and villages to the west we came across more and more communities of displaced Dinkas. They were working as share-croppers or day labourers or domestic servants. In the larger Dinka settlements in Darfur, where Mark worked, the dry season had brought a water problem. In a village of four or five thousand people with a single functioning water pump, a sudden increase in the population could be counted on to provoke a crisis, one made worse by the local attitudes to Dinkas—unbelievers, slaves—which meant that they were always last in line, after cattle and camels. We saw them waiting all morning for the nomadic Baggara to water their herds.

It was hard to avoid hearing stories of atrocities committed by the Arab militias. This woman had been raped; this man tortured and castrated; that man's wife had been killed in front of him; a boy of ten had been kidnapped and kept for two years as a servant, beaten when he tried to escape, finally killed. There were clearly many Dinkas still in captivity.

Five days after we left Khartoum we arrived at Mark's base in Ed Da'ein. There we heard over the radio that a medical team had finally managed to get to Abyei. There were four expatriates—a doctor and three nurses—and a number of volunteers from the Sudan Red Crescent. It had taken six months, from May, when Carol Berger's article appeared, until October, for relief agencies to mount an operation in Abyei. For the last two months the Red Cross had a transport plane ready to fly, a Hercules standing at Khartoum airport. Oxfam and the Save The Children

Following page: Khartoum

Fund had nurses on stand-by; there was a doctor from Médecins Sans Frontières waiting to leave. Grain was stored in sheds at the airport. In October the relief agencies had concluded an agreement with the government—or so they thought. When they got to Abyei they were turned back at the airstrip; the army commander refused to let them disembark. They tried again; they were turned back again.

I had spoken to Carol Berger before I left England. She told me I shouldn't go. Relief agencies in the Sudan were compromised, she said, because they worked through the government. It was the government that had created the problem they were supposed to solve. Now it was using the agencies to save face, and because it needed relief supplies to feed its own forces. Food was a weapon; Abyei was a war zone. Without official recognition of this, the agencies were giving legitimacy to a government that was betraying its own citizens. 'It's a wicked business, John,' said Carol. 'You wait and see.'

Were the issues as stark as this? Over the radio from Khartoum we learned of the difficulties facing the members of the relief team. They had finally been allowed to stay in Abyei, but there were restrictions. They had no radio transmitter so they could not communicate with Khartoum except when a plane came. They were confined to the hospital and not allowed to move around the town, so they had no way of knowing the extent of the malnutrition and disease they were dealing with. They were not permitted even to observe the distribution of the food that was coming in on the Red Cross plane. Nor were the Red Cross officials.

The next day we set out for Abyei by way of Babanusa, a railway junction in Kordofan where some of the survivors of El Meiram had ended up. Before leaving, Mark's drivers insisted on an initiation rite for his Land Rover. He was instructed to sacrifice a sheep and dip his hands in the blood, then make handprints all over the white bodywork. The effect was striking, as though a violent crime had taken place. In this curious livery we set out on the last leg of our journey.

Photo (preceding pages): Nancy Nash (Frank Spooner)

There were dwarf baobabs in bloom, silvery and obese, and arboreal pachyderms wreathed in pink. A red-bark acacia exploded with white doves. At a town called Kilekli we stopped to watch blacksmiths in the market place. Their hammers glinted in the sun. They had cannibalized abandoned trucks; now they were beating steel leaf-springs into broadswords.

We stopped briefly at some of the towns where the militias were said to congregate: Abu Matariq, whose name means Anvil, from slavery days; Abu Gabra, where we talked to two Dinkas looking for their sons, who had been abducted by militiamen. We bypassed Tibbun, where, it was rumoured, a weekly slave market had been established.

We arrived at Babanusa at midday.

The survivors of El Meiram were living under plastic sheeting and in abandoned boxcars on railway sidings. Most of them had walked seventy miles to a camp at El Muglad, then a further twenty to Babanusa, hoping to get a train eastwards, out of the hunger zone. Some of them were waiting in the hope of being reunited with their families. In El Meiram desperate parents had given their children away—or sold them—to Arabs as cow and goat herds. Or they had simply been kidnapped. They could be ransomed, or they would be sold as slaves.

There was a camp for the displaced Dinkas, but we were not allowed to speak to them; smiling security men escorted us away. I managed to talk to a medical assistant in the grass-roofed clinic where he and two nurses were trying to minister to thousands of malnourished adults and children. As we spoke a woman gave birth. Her child was still-born. They brought it to her wrapped in a white cotton shawl. When she saw it was dead, she would not touch it; she rolled over to face the wall. Half an hour later she was dead too.

There were boxcars in Babanusa loaded with EEC-donated grain destined for Aweil. The grain had been there for more than a year. The SPLA was known to attack railway convoys on the grounds that they were supplying ammunition to government

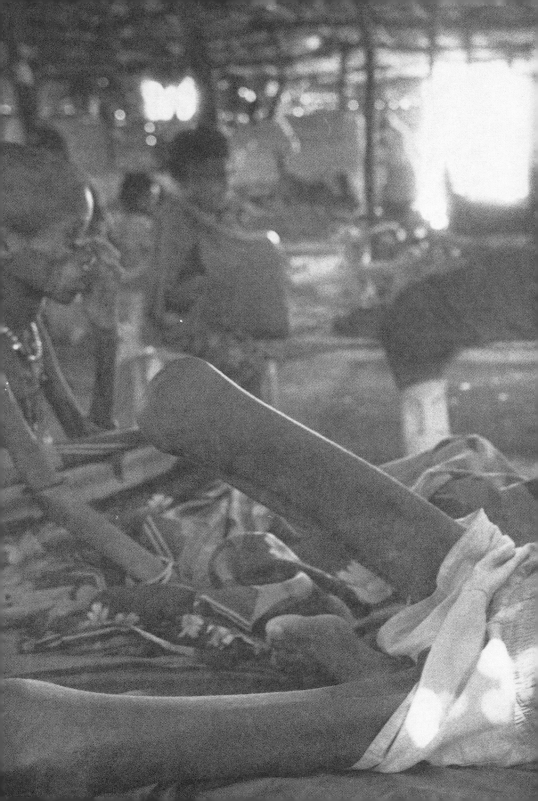

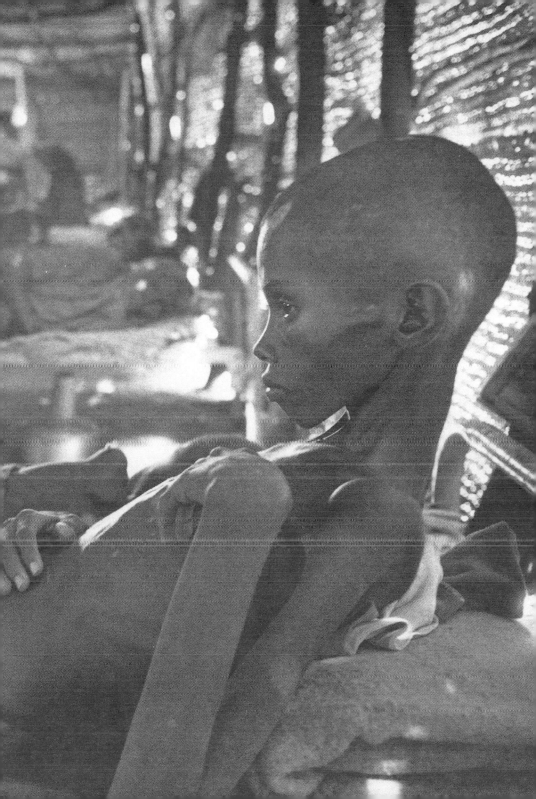

garrisons, instead of food to the people, and the grain cars were ostensibly still waiting for an army escort. But supply trains from Babanusa were passing through El Meiram every month on their way to the army garrison on the Bahr-el-Arab.

A railway worker told us about the trains. The relief grain that arrived in Babanusa and El Muglad was habitually commandeered by local government officials. Some would go to the army; some would turn up for sale in the market.

'Why should they let food go to the Dinkas,' he said, 'when they are hungry themselves?'

It was to be another two months before a train got through to Aweil. Eight thousand people died in the town during the rains. It was clear that it was not only in Abyei that famine relief was subordinated to what government officials referred to as security considerations. There was something bad happening in Kordofan. Greed, the evil of war, the legacy of slavery. Carol had been right: it was a wicked business.

SOUTH-WEST SUDAN

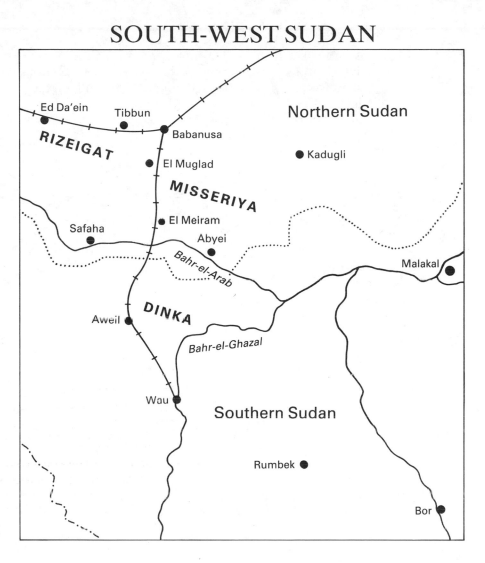

RIZEIGAT

Ed Da'ein
Tibbun
Babanusa

Northern Sudan

Kadugli

El Muglad

MISSERIYA

Safaha

El Meiram

Abyei

Bahr-el-Arab

Malakal

DINKA

Aweil

Bahr-el-Ghazal

Wau

Southern Sudan

Rumbek

Bor

Supping with the Devil in El Muglad

The next day we drove to El Muglad, the heart of Humr Misseriya territory. Here the road to Abyei meets the road to El Meiram. It was the last place where there was any semblance of civil, as opposed to military, administration. As in Babanusa there was a large camp of displaced Dinkas by the railway. In Babanusa we had been forbidden to speak to them; in El Muglad we were not even allowed to visit the camp.

There was one relief agency in El Muglad. We arrived there at an awkward moment. The agency had arranged a supper party for local dignitaries, but that morning an order had come from Khartoum expelling all foreign relief workers from Southern Kordofan. It looked as though their soirée might turn out to be an envoi—for us too. But their field officer, a genial Irishman, was unphazed, and, by lunch-time, the expulsion order had been revoked.

The field officer had a certain fame. At a time when no one was able to enter Abyei, he had succeeded in getting 500 sacks of dura into the town—in the rainy season, on donkeys, having hired local militiamen to ride shotgun. He made no bones about it: nothing moved between El Muglad and Abyei without their say so. The priest in Abyei had sent him a message: dozens of Dinkas were dying every day. The only way to help them was to employ the same militias who had driven them from their homes. It was a heightened version of the dilemma facing all the relief organizations. The field officer knew where he stood.

'They're killers, aren't they, the militias?' I asked.

'Of course,' he said, stroking his beard. 'So are the SPLA.' And then he added: 'I'd sup with the devil to get food to Abyei.'

At dusk the guests arrived for the field officer's party.

In the yard of the house, under the mango trees, a long table was laid with food and flowers, and easy chairs made of bright nylon cord were arranged in a square.

On one side of the square sat the Misseriya elders in snow-white *jallabias*, with fine cotton scarves thrown over their shoulders

Opposite: Food line at a relief agency camp in the South.

and turbans perched on their heads like whipped cream. They clutched heavy walking sticks and murmured to their neighbours while waiting to eat. On the other side sat the agency staff. Government officials in western dress were on the third side—the chiefs of police from Babanusa and Abyei, the army commander and the head of military security in El Muglad. Next to the head of military security, and engaged in intimate conversation, was a small man in a pale-coloured safari suit. He was also clutching a walking stick. The field officer pointed him out to me. 'That is the head of the Misseriya militia,' he said. 'Al Capone. Mr Big. If he says "Kill", they kill.'

Between Mr Big and the head of military security was an Arab trader with a gold tooth and an ingratiating smile. This was Mr Fixit, the go-between with the militiamen. Majak recognized him. Gold-tooth had grown up in Abyei. 'He was just a truck driver then,' said Majak. But it seemed he had grown rich on famine. It was he who had arranged the agency donkey train to Abyei. He owned many houses in El Muglad, including the one we were sitting in. We were, in a sense, his guests. Mark mentioned to him that we were planning to go to Abyei the next day, and soon Gold-tooth was arranging an escort for us. There was a whispered conversation and a nod from Mr Big.

'We'll protect you against the SPLA,' he said warmly. But we knew the SPLA was not the problem on the road to Abyei—it was not from them we needed protection: it was from the militiamen themselves. Nevertheless, Gold-tooth was very persuasive, and by the end of the conversation Mark and I found we had arranged to meet him for breakfast the next day to pick up an escort.

A nervous young northerner was circulating among the guests, a journalist on a Khartoum paper, *Senabil*, the voice of the fundamentalist Islamic Front. He wandered about with a Nikon camera round his neck, but never used it. He was a Misseri from Tibbun, where the slave market was supposed to be, and since he was a journalist, I felt it was reasonable to ask him about the market. He moved aside so that no one could hear.

'What is going on is *bad*,' he said. 'But you have to remember we are tribal people. All of us—Arab, Dinka—everyone. Even I—I am a Muslim, but I am also a Misseri. I practice *rituals* that are not Muslim at all. There is a tradition to everything we do, a *subtext*, a tribal subtext.'

'Really?' I said, startled by the salon language, but aware that he had not answered my question.

'Yes,' said the journalist, 'my people are Arabs. But they are Africans also. It is their way. They come out of the forest on horses. They think everyone is their slave. When they take cattle it is not just for them, it is for the good of the tribe. They are not thieves, they are—what is the phrase?'

'Social bandits?' I said.

'Yes, yes,' said the journalist. 'Sociable bandits.'

At that moment the only other expatriate in El Muglad arrived, a British employee of Chevron, the oil company that has the lion's share of the concessions in the southern Sudan. He was wearing a white T-shirt with a red inscription. In the twilight I could not quite make it out. One of the Misseriya elders gave it an uncomprehending glance.

The journalist studied it intently. 'What does that say?' he asked.

I looked again. On the chest of the man from Chevron were the words 'Fuck the World with Yuppie Condoms.'

I said something about it being a tribal subtext, but I wasn't sure if the journalist got the joke. I wasn't sure if I got it myself. In the circumstances literary theory and the delinquent language of T-shirts both seemed obscene. Words had come unhinged from events; people took refuge in subtexts and incomprehensible slogans. I thought about our car with its bloody handprints, about the Misseriya elders with their beautiful white clothes, about slaves and social bandits, yuppie condoms, gold teeth. Bloodstains. The milk of birds. I felt stoned. I thought about what was happening in the South, just south of here, behind this screen of lies. Burning, looting, pillage, killing, torture, rape, starvation. I thought about the massacre in Ed Da'ein the year before. Such things could happen again. I tried to remember why I had come, why I had imagined there was anything I could usefully do or say about these terrible things. I felt sick.

The Road to Abyei

In the morning Mark and I woke with the same feeling. We had gone too far: we felt ashamed in front of Majak; arriving in Abyei under the protection of the militia was not the right way to begin. We drove to breakfast discussing how we could get out of the arrangement, but in the event the trader was all smiles and shrugs. On our heads be it. It was clear he reckoned that any transport operation we set up would require his services in the end. He wrote a letter of recommendation for us to a fellow-trader in Abyei. As we talked, a police sergeant stepped into his shop, looked around and exchanged a word with him. The policeman left with a fifty-pound note. Gold-tooth winked and sighed. 'Their salaries are so low,' he said. As we got up to leave we saw the leader of the militia, the sociable bandit, crossing the street; we moved away rapidly and drove out of town.

We followed the railway south of Abyei past pools of lotus flowers. To cross the watercourses, still deep with mud, we had to straddle the tracks and bump along the cross-ties. After a few miles, we branched west, hoping we had chosen the right road. There were no other vehicles. An Arab rode ahead of us on a donkey, a huge rusty spear under his arm. He looked like Don Quixote, an anachronism from the age before submachine guns changed the rules of the game.

The road worsened and our progress was slow. There were Dinka boys herding cattle and goats. One was malnourished and needed a stick to walk. He was about six years old. We stopped to speak to him. His mother, he said, had given him to an Arab because she had no food. We drove on. Two boys in rags froze when they saw our car. We stopped and Majak got out and spoke to them in Dinka. They told him they were brothers; the elder was nine, the younger five; they were running away from their Arab master and trying to rejoin their mother in El Muglad. They did not know what had become of their father. We gave them food and money, but their chances of making it without being recaptured were not too good.

Further ahead, we saw another group of men under some trees. They also were on donkeys, but instead of spears they carried GM3 rifles, a type used by the Army. They were not in uniform.

They motioned us to stop and we did so. I stowed my camera. Mark kept his foot poised over the accelerator. They asked where we had come from but they did not ask about the boys we had just spoken to. They peered in the back of the car and stared at the bloody handprints on the body-work. Then they waved us on.

We were entering what had once been Dinka territory. There were deserted villages with rusting water tanks and unused pumps; there were charred huts, and fields reclaimed by the bush. The vegetation was lusher and the woods thicker but many trees had been burned in forest fires. The evening sky grew dark, and we entered Abyei. The town looked eerie, swathed in smoke from cooking fires, with a faint glow on the trees as though the undergrowth was alight.

Following page: Dinka goatherds in the South.

Photo: Hutchison Library   Photo (preceding pages): Chip Hires (Frank Spooner)

W e had arrived. Just as we passed the first buildings, a soldier in camouflage ran from the shadows. *'Sebit!'* he shouted, 'Halt !' He crouched down in the road with his rifle pointing at the windscreen. Mark doused the headlights and switched on the cabin light. The sentry demanded a password that we did not have. He asked where we had come from. There was only one place we could have come from. And there was only one place he could take us to. We drove on with him to the police post.

In Kordofan you are not supposed to arrive anywhere after dark. In Abyei it was rare for anyone to arrive at all. We did not know if the authorities had been advised of our departure from El Muglad, but it would not have been unusual if the message had not got through. In the event the police were perfectly civil. They took us to a nearby compound where the medical team were staying. Most of the team were asleep outside. Their mosquito nets shone in the moonlight like sails in harbour. The policemen, off-duty in their long white *jallabias*, glided like pleasure-craft among them. For the moment we were glad to anchor there.

The Harvest of Skulls

In the morning Mark and I registered formally with the chief of police. To our surprise, he gave us permission to move around the town. A soldier accompanied us.

The army had burned the huts to the south of the town to discourage infiltration by the SPLA, and we were not allowed to go there. We could see a bare mound under a tree, the grave of a former Paramount Chief of the Ngok. Close to the airstrip there was the army compound, and beyond the airstrip were the ruins of the Harvard Project, an ill-fated scheme that was supposed to have made Abyei into a model of integrated rural development for the Sudan.

Opposite: Dinkas building a hut.

Following page: Refugees in an abandoned schoolyard, Juba.

John Ryle

Abyei is a small town in normal times: a market place, a street of shops, three schools, the airstrip and a sprawl of grass huts. It has a dry season population of about 5,000. That 5,000 is composed of Dinka villagers, government administrators and Arab traders. It is the administrative centre for the Ngok—in normal times. It is also a market town for other Dinka tribes from the South. It was these tribes who now formed the majority of the displaced population of the town. The dry season is the busy time in a place like Abyei: the harvest is over and people move between the surrounding villages and the cattle camps near the rivers; the rivers are low and travelling is easier. People come and go from October until April when the rains come again and planting begins.

But 1988, of course, had not been a normal year. Plenty of people left their villages to come to Abyei, but few went back. The seasonal movement had become one-way. The buildings of the town had diminished—the army having burned whole sections to the ground—but the population itself had tripled or quadrupled. It had been even larger in the months before we arrived, but malnutrition and disease had taken their toll. The rains had been plentiful, but the harvest had been pitiful—no one dared risk attacks from the militia. The only good thing was that the rains had brought fish. The dry season is the fishing season, and, in Abyei, fish had very likely saved more lives than relief agencies.

We walked through the centre of the town. There was a scattering of brick and cement buildings—schools commandeered by the army. The *suq*, the food market, was virtually empty; there were a few traders. In the crowded huts behind the *suq* lived the famine victims. Not everyone looked hungry: the worst cases were hidden. In many of the huts were sick children and old people, their skin in folds. One struggled to rise to her feet to greet us but she failed. They could not get to the hospital; the medical workers were forbidden to go to them.

In the hospital we found the medical team. It was administering the MUAC test—measuring children's middle and upper arm circumference—to discover the incidence of malnutrition. The children were given coloured wristbands to identify them as participants in the supplementary feeding programme. They got a mixture of dried skimmed milk, sugar and cereal called Unimix, brewed up in oil drums over charcoal fires in the hospital grounds. The hospital had no water supply. That also came in drums from the pump near the airstrip.

All over the town were children with pencil legs and balloon bellies wearing those tiny wristbands. They wore them like jewellery. Some had nothing else to wear. Some of them were too weak to walk and had to be carried by their siblings a mile or more from their huts to the hospital. Many had perpetual diarrhoea. Weak children are wiped out very quickly by diarrhoea. In the hospital they were given rehydration fluid, with one measure of salt to half-a-dozen of sugar; the measuring spoon bore this inscription: 'Do Not Use If More Salty Than Tears.'

Following page: Displaced Dinkas queueing for water.

John Ryle

There were few men under the age of forty in Abyei. Among the Dinkas there were only women and children and old men to be seen. The young men had been killed by soldiers or by militiamen, or they had stayed deep in the bush with the remaining cattle, or they had joined the SPLA. But as we walked among the huts near the *suq* we were startled by half-a-dozen tall youths, bare-chested, sleek and healthy, with red berets and guns, who strode past us looking straight ahead. The youths did not acknowledge us or return our greeting—until we spoke to them in Nuer, the language of a Nilotic tribe to the east of the Ngok. They were, we established, members of another government-backed militia, Anyanya II. Most of Anyanya II had abandoned the government side and gone over to the SPLA, but not these ones. They had been driven out by the SPLA and had fallen back on Abyei. The Nuer and their families had safe passes from the government. In one section of the town they had even set up a machine-gun emplacement. It was pointing directly into the market place. The Nuer boys had exploited their position to loot the displaced Dinka. They had stolen all the fishing nets. In the whole town only the Nuer and a few Arab traders had cattle. It was a complicated war.

We were forbidden from visiting the church in Abyei, but in the open space in front of the barracks we met a Catholic father, the Italian priest who had alerted the relief people in El Muglad to the situation in Abyei earlier that year. At the height of the famine, he told us, he had fed 7,000 people in one day. 'Beats Jesus,' I murmured. Then I felt ashamed, because the priest was old and ill. Luckily he was also very deaf. He told us that the local church representative on the food distribution committee in Abyei had been arrested and the church, which arranged the relief supplies, was now prevented from distributing them.

We spent the night with the medical team again, and in the morning accompanied members of the Red Crescent on a burial detail. On the north-east side of the town there was a field of skulls. Corpses had been thrown there in the last months of the rains when the grass was tall. Now the grass was pale and dry. It had died down to reveal the shame of people too weary and ill to bury their dead. Vultures and hyenas had spread the remains far and wide. The Red Crescent volunteers, northerners, collecting the scattered bones to bury them in a single grave, made much of this. 'We even gave them money to bury their dead,' said the team leader, a doctor, 'but they took the money and left the corpses in the grass.'

'What would you have done?' I asked, 'if you got money when you were starving? Wouldn't you feed the living first?'

The Red Crescent doctor turned back to the bones. The volunteers had dug a very shallow pit. The bones would soon be gnawed out of their graves again.

I walked across the plain with Majak counting skulls and noting the size of the skeletons. Adults and children seemed to be represented in equal numbers; on one skull the tribal marks of the Dinka tribe to the south were faintly visible—four lines across the forehead in a broad V-shape, gouged to the bone in early adolescence. Tiny zig-zag cracks flickered across the cranium like stream-beds on an extinct volcano. Everywhere there were bones. In the distance women came out of the woods with bundles of grass and firewood on their heads. It was a glimpse of normality. Famine or no famine, in Africa it is women who do the work.

A glimpse was all we got of the situation in Abyei. Someone had been talking to the chief of police and overnight he became distinctly sour. 'Why are you here?' he kept asking us. 'We do not know why you are here.' In the end he turned to me. 'You will have to leave on the next plane,' he said. I suppose Majak might have asked the chief of police the same question—why was he

Following page: A southern village in the dry season.

there?—but he did not. He had come back to find his home town half burned to the ground and under military occupation. He was in the habit of self-control. He told me he was trying to think of Abyei as another place altogether, a place where he had not been before.

'Why are you here?' I couldn't really answer the question in a way that would have satisfied the police chief. I was there to assess the effectiveness of the relief programme. But the authorities in Abyei did not seem to think that it was a relief agency's job to assess its own programme, or, for that matter, even to administer it. In particular they did not think it was an agency's job to know anything about the people it was trying to help—especially if those people were Dinkas, causing the government so much grief and dying in such embarrassing numbers.

More and more in the Sudan the most valuable function of relief agencies has come to be to protect people from their own government. The government does not take kindly to this.

In fact, the worst seemed to be over in Abyei. What we saw was not famine, but its aftermath. Maybe five or ten people a day were dying when we arrived. Some of the food sent to Abyei—not most, but some—had reached the needy. And some of the medicines had been used to treat the sick. As late-comers to the famine we were seeing the survivors. It was oddly uplifting. These were people who had experienced terrible deprivation, yet they had made it. Most of those who had stayed alive would recover if the relief programme continued. Majak and I discussed the need for fishing nets to replace those that had been stolen by the Nuer militiamen. On our last day, Mark talked to the nurses about reorganizing the hospital.

The plane was due in the morning. We had one more night in Abyei. After nightfall we were supposed to be confined to our quarters, but the Red Crescent doctor was on good terms with the military and insisted that I accompany him to see the Dinkas

Photo (preceding pages): Sarah Errington (Hutchison Library)

dancing. 'Their culture is very primitive,' he said, 'but it is interesting to observe.' It was the tribal subtext again. The same distancing language.

I went with the doctor to the dancing ground; the moonlight glittered on the river, but the dance was a lacklustre affair. I had seen better in the shanty towns in Khartoum. There were a few dozen girls, but no young men to dance with them. The army commander arrived with his bodyguard. It seemed that he, too, had an interest in primitive culture or possibly he had an interest in us.

I walked back to our compound hand in hand with the Red Crescent doctor. 'You know,' he said, 'with all these Dinka and these Dinka-Nuer coming here, the SPLA has done us a great favour by driving them out of the South. Before long they will all be Muslims—'

'Do you really think so?' I said.

'Yes. They will all be Muslims and then we shall have solved our country's problems. There will be no North and South. You wait and see.'

This was the Islamic Front's view of the future, of the unifying force of Islam, the submersion of tribal cultures, at least of non-Muslim tribal cultures, in religious brotherhood. A cloak, dissident northerners would say, for the continuing economic domination of the country by sectional interests in Khartoum.

'Well,' said the Red Crescent doctor, 'tell me. What else can unify the country?'

There was no easy answer. There are no easy answers to anything in Sudan. It is a complicated war. An impossible country. Talking to the northern doctor I sensed, beneath the Panglossian strain, a desperate desire to believe that Sudan could really function as a country, that it could become a nation, with a government that could see beyond tomorrow. No North, no South . . . all Muslim. In moments of weariness it was possible to wonder whether this might not be better than an endless war. But a Baggara blitzkrieg was hardly the way to persuade anyone of the benefits of embracing Islam, or of its role in state formation.

Following page: Sudan People's Liberation Army Guerrillas.

At midday the drone of engines became audible through the haze. Soon we could see the Hercules circling round the town. It came in to land. Unloading the plane took no time at all—the plane only carried 150 sacks of grain, hardly more than fit on the back of a lorry. The runway at Abyei was too short to permit a full load. Supplying the town by air was sensationally expensive. Shipping us out in the empty plane cost nothing at all.

In the Belly of the Hercules

The belly of the Hercules was bare. Grains of dura from leaky sacks rolled on the floor like ball-bearings. There were only five passengers. Through the tiny window we could see the Bahr-el-Arab, the border between North and South, twisting through the grass. Like a fish, like fire, like the cracks on a skull. Below us was the dancing ground. Beyond it were the killing fields of the South. The land was flat and brown, the colour of tanned hide; Robert Maker was buried somewhere there—or perhaps the hyenas had got him too.

This was the stretch of land where I had mislaid the tribal boundary a decade before, the 4,000 square miles I had pored over in the map office in Khartoum. This was the edge of the southern plain, where the surveyors, Major Titherington and his ilk, had roamed in the 1920s and 1930s. For centuries before, the Nilotic tribes had lived and moved here without maps, without benefit of modernity, without a state, without a religion of the book; with only their land and their cattle and their own society. Their territory stretched below us, a realm of conflict and disorder. Without their land, without cattle, could the Dinka survive as a people? What future was there? A drifting sub-proletariat, ship-wrecked on the periphery of some northern city, trapped in shanty towns, in Hillat

Kusha, the place of garbage, another pastoral people on the rubbish tip of history.

It was cold in the plane. Twilight outside, no lights below. Next to me Majak was deep in thought.

'Imagine,' he said, 'if peace comes.'

I tried. I imagined the displaced Dinka repossessing their land, restoring their depleted herds, driving their guns into the ground as cattle pegs, bathing in the silver rivers of the South, growing sleek on the milk of the rainy season.

I remembered again the day Robert Maker and I went to Karic. It was peaceful and cool, a perfect day in July; the rains were slack and the ground-nuts ripening. The road was red with mud; our wheels slipped, and we both fell off our bicycles. On the road we passed a stream where girls were bathing and cart-wheeling in the shade of a fig tree. We slipped into the water on the other side and watched them, lurking like crocodiles in the reed beds.

There was a dance in a village hidden in the woods to the north; we could hear the drum. On the road young men walked hand in hand, their faces and limbs zebra-striped with clay and ash, wearing brass and ivory bracelets on their arms and legs and fantastic turbans on their heads. They sang *kêêp* and *wuak*, songs composed in the fattening camps, where they had been drinking milk since the rains began. They were songs in praise of oxen, paeans to their red-nosed Makuci, whose hide was the colour of the fish-eagle's wings, or Marial with the black-tasselled horn. Later, in Karic, some elders sang an old war-song, *kong*, full of the hyperbolic threats that are characteristic of the genre:

John Ryle

My ox Mayom is fearless
  He is fearless

My spear is red with blood
We sacrifice to the spirit of the men of Dor
When the moon waxes and when it has waned,
In battle we attack again and again
Until the earth is all ploughed up
  The earth is all ploughed up

I am a bull, hated by the enemy
The enemy will be destroyed
If I use only half my strength
If I am far from home
Still they will be destroyed
  They will be destroyed

Adel, what has made the people so angry?
They are as strong as a python
And they are making sacrifices
  I speared the ox Makuei in Wunrol
  Our generation grinds men into dust

If we hate a thing
  We hate it
If we are at peace
  We let it be

We spent the evening transcribing and translating these songs by the light of a paraffin lamp in Robert's uncle's house. Robert was very good at this. Much of what I understood about the Dinkas, their intransigence and bravado, I owed to him. *If we hate a thing, we hate it*. This tendency to favour the open expression of disagreement has led the Dinka and other southern tribes into a conflict where the weapons and the rhetoric are very different. Mines and machine-guns have replaced spears and clubs; the language of national liberation is superimposed on that of tribal loyalty. Modernity has come to the Dinkas through the barrel of a gun. How much of the village life I had recorded with Robert's help will survive the harsh dislocations and cryptic violence of the present time? Hundreds of thousands of Dinkas have been displaced by the war; tens of thousands have lost their lives. Other southern tribes are similarly affected. Cattle-rich pastoralists have been transformed into landless labourers, without rights or possessions; villagers who have never seen a town before struggle to survive in the cities of the North. On the other side, school boys recruited into a guerrilla army are taught to live by the gun, their minds filled with revolutionary slogans as dubious as the propaganda of the Islamic Front. Whoever won, much would be lost.

John Ryle

S udan lives on foreign aid. The bulk of it comes from the United States. The United States might seem an odd bedfellow for an Islamicizing regime of the kind presently in power, but *rapprochement* between the rebels and western powers is hindered by the fact that the SPLA's main support comes from the Stalinist regime of Ethiopia, a country with a grim civil war of its own. As I left Sudan, the government, through the United Nations, was about to launch a seventy million dollar appeal for assistance with its most besetting problem, the displaced southerners, an estimated million and a half of them. Forty-five dollars per southerner. The proposals were on the desk of every aid official in Khartoum. Nowhere was it pointed out that the problem of the displaced in the North was largely of the government's own making.

For strategic reasons the government of the Sudan has sponsored the extermination of a segment of its own civilian population. Many thousands of people have been killed by government militias; thousands more have died as a result of their raids; and thousands, probably, have been disenfranchised, held in servitude by members of those militias hand-in-glove with government forces. Not thousands, but hundreds of thousands— some say millions—have been rendered homeless and destitute as a result of the conflict. The government is not about to acknowledge responsibility for its part in this catastrophe. It falls to others to point this out. That was why we had to leave Abyei.

In February 1989, Abyei came under attack by the SPLA and the western relief agencies withdrew their personnel. Without them there, more people will undoubtedly die. And without them there it will be that much harder to get any information, to know how many people are dying. Soon the rains will come again, the hungriest time of the year. More destitute villagers will be arriving in Abyei and in other border towns, seeking food and security—and peace that does not come.

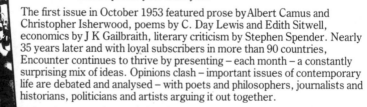

BRUCE CHATWIN
1940 TO 1989
THE BEY

A mong my first jobs at Sotheby's was that of porter in the Department of Greek and Roman Antiquities. Whenever there was a sale I would put on my grey porter's uniform and stand behind the glass vitrines, making sure that prospective buyers didn't sticky the objects with their fingers.

One morning there appeared an elderly and anachronistic gentleman in a black, astrakhan-collared coat, carrying a black, silver-tipped cane. His syrupy eyes and brushed-up moustache announced him as a relic of the Ottoman Empire.

'Can you show me something beautiful?' he asked. 'Greek, *not* Roman!'

'I think I can,' I said.

I showed him a fragment of an Attic white-ground *lekythos* by the Achilles Painter which had the most refined drawing, in golden-sepia, of a naked boy. It had come from the collection of Lord Elgin.

'Ha!' said the old gentleman. 'I see you have The Eye. I too have The Eye. We shall be friends.'

He handed me his card. I watched the black coat recede into the gallery:

PAUL A . . . F . . . BEY
GRAND CHAMBERLAIN DU COUR DU ROI DES ALBANIS

'So,' I said to myself. 'Zog's Chamberlain.'

He was true to his word. We became friends. He would turn up in London on some business of Albanians in exile. He fretted about Queen Geraldine in Estoril. He regretted that King Leka in Madrid had to earn his living in real estate.

He spoke of the works of art that had been his. He had sold his fauvist Braques and paintings by Juan Gris *en bloc* to the Australian art collector, Douglas Cooper. He spoke of the excellent pheasant-shooting in his ancestral domain. He had never been to Albania but had spent his life between Switzerland and Alexandria. Did I know, he once asked, that the government of Enver Hoxha was a homosexual cabal?

'At least, that's what they tell me.'

I soon realized that the Bey was not a buyer but a seller. His straitened circumstances forced him from time to time to dispense

with a work of art. Would I, he inquired rather sheepishly, be interested in acquiring some odds and ends from his collection?

'I certainly would,' I said.

'Perhaps I could show you a few things at the Ritz?'

I had next to no money. The Directors at Sotheby's assumed that people like myself had private incomes to supplement our wretched salaries. What was I to do? Exist on air? I earned myself a little extra by trafficking in antiquities—until the Chairman told me to stop. It was wrong for members of the staff to deal in works of art because they actively hindered a possible sale at auction.

I felt this was unfair. The Chairman himself was the biggest dealer of all.

But with the Bey my conscience was clear. He refused to sell anything at auction. I don't think he could bear the idea of his things being handled on viewing day by *hoi polloi*, by people who did *not* have The Eye. Besides, he gave me everything as a present. Spread out over his bed at the Ritz would be a cluster of exquisite objects: an Archaic Greek bronze, a fragment of Mosan *chasse*, a Byzantine cameo, an Egyptian green slate palette of pre-dynastic period, and many others.

'Would you like them?' he asked anxiously.

'I would.'

'In that case I give them to you! Between two friends who have The Eye there can be no question of money.'

I would wrap the treasures in tissue-paper and, taking them to a dealer friend, find out how much I could get for them. I always tried to keep one or two for myself.

A day later the phone would ring. 'Chatwin, could you spare a few moments to have a drink with me?'

'Of course I could, Bey.'

We would meet in the Ritz Bar.

'Chatwin, I've one or two little favours to ask you. You know how tiresome it is to move funds around Europe. Banks are so unobliging these days. I find I've overspent on this visit. I wonder if you could settle a few things for me.'

'Of course, Bey.'

'I've been a bit extravagant at the tailor. Three or four suits. Four pairs of shoes at Lobb. And there's the poor old Bentley! She had to have a new radiator.'

'I'll see what I can do,' I said.

I went to the tailor and asked for the Bey's bill. I went to Lobb. I discovered from Jack Barclay the cost of the radiator. The Bey's prices were never excessive; but, in the best oriental tradition, we always had a haggle at the end. Otherwise, the deal would not be a deal.

'Chatwin, I wonder if you could have a word with the Ritz cashier? I thought of leaving for Switzerland on Saturday week.'

'Out of the question, Bey. I suggest this Monday.'

'Alas, that cannot be. On Tuesday Lady Turnbull is giving a cocktail for the Anglo-Albanian Society. As Chamberlain, I have to attend.'

'Wednesday then?'

'Wednesday it shall be.'

'And no more phone calls after today?'

'The telephone is entirely mine.'

This went on for two or three years. Nowadays, I sometimes thumb through the catalogues of an American museum, or an exhibition of ancient art, and there, illustrated full-plate, will be an object or a painting that passed from the Bey to myself: 'a unique Cycladic marble vessel . . .', 'a Pentellic marble head of a youth from a late fifth-century Attic stele . . .', 'a white marble head of a Putto, attributed to Desiderio di Settignano . . .', 'a painting of Christ Mocked, in tempera on linen, by a follower of Mantegna, possibly by Melozzo da Forlì . . .'

We have one object left from the Bey's collection: my wife's engagement ring. It is a Greek electrum ring of the late fifth century B.C. The Bey bought it in 1947 from a Cairo dealer called Tano. I believe it comes from the Tell-el Mashkuta Treasure, most of which is now in the Brooklyn Museum.

The intaglio has a wounded lioness levering with her mouth and forepaw the hunter's spear from her flank. Not entirely suitable as an engagement present, but I think it the loveliest Greek ring I ever saw.

I write about the Bey because people of his kind will never come again. His life, I suspect, was a bit of a sham. The Eye was always young and pure.

BRUCE CHATWIN
MRS MANDELSTAM

Bruce Chatwin

It was snowing hard the afternoon I went to see Nadezhda Mandelstam. The snow melted off my coat and boots and made puddles on her kitchen floor. The kitchen smelled of kerosene and stale bread. On a table there were sticky purple rings made by a dishcloth printed with a map of Queensland hung from a hook on the door, a begonia and a jug of dried grasses left over from the lightness of a Russian summer.

A fat man in spectacles came out of the bedroom. He glared at me as he wound a grey scarf around his jowls, and then went out.

She called me in. She lay on her left side, on her bed, amid the rumpled sheets, resting her temple on a clenched fist. She greeted me without moving.

'What did you think of my doctor?' she sneered. 'I am sick.'

The doctor, I assume, was her KGB man.

The room was hot and cramped and strewn with clothes and books. Her hair was coarse, like lichen, and the light from the bedside lamp shone through it. White metal fastenings glittered among the brown stumps of her teeth. A cigarette stuck to her lower lip. Her nose was a weapon. You knew for certain she was one of the most powerful women in the world, and knew she knew it.

A friend in England advised me to take her three things: champagne, cheap thrillers and marmalade. She looked at the champagne and said, 'Bollinger!' without enthusiasm. She looked at the thrillers and said *'Romans policiers*! Next time you come to Moscow you must bring me real *trash*!' But when I pulled out three jars of my mother's Seville orange marmalade, she stubbed out the cigarette and smiled.

'Thank you, my dear. Marmalade, it is my childhood.'

'Tell me, my dear . . .' she waved me to a chair and, as she waved, one of her breasts tumbled out of her nightie. 'Tell me,' she shoved it back, 'are there any grand poets left in your country? I mean grand poets . . . of the stature of Joyce or Eliot?'

Auden was alive, in Oxford. Weakly, I suggested Auden.

'Auden is *not* what I would call a grand poet!'

'Yes,' I said. 'Most of the voices are silent.'

'And in prose?'

'Not much.'

114

'And in America? Are there poets?'

'Some.'

'Tell me, was Hemingway a grand novelist?'

'Not always,' I said. 'Not towards the end. But he's underrated now. The early short stories are wonderful.'

'But the wonderful American novelist is Faulkner. I am helping a young friend translate Faulkner into Russian. I must tell you, we are having difficulties.

'And in Russia,' she growled, 'we have no grand writers left. Here also the voices are silent. We have Solzhenitsyn and even that is not so good. The trouble with Solzhenitsyn is this. When he thinks he is telling the truth, he tells the most terrible falsehoods. But when he thinks he is making a story from his imagination, then, sometimes, he catches the truth.'

'What about that story . . .' I faltered. 'I forget its name . . . the one where the old woman gets run over by a train?'

'You mean "Matryona's House"?'

'I do,' I said. 'Does that catch the truth?'

'It could never have happened in Russia!'

On the wall across from the bed there was a white canvas, hung askew. The painting was all white, white on white, a few white bottles on a blank white ground. I knew the work of the artist: a Ukrainian Jew, like herself.

'I see you've got a painting by Weissberg,' I said.

'Yes. And I wonder if you'd mind straightening it for me? I threw a book and hit it by mistake. A disgusting book by an Australian woman!'

I straightened the picture.

'Weissberg,' she said. 'He is our best painter. Perhaps that is all one can do today in Russia? Paint whiteness!'

I n January 1973, on a morning of Stygian gloom, I called
on Konstantin Melnikov, the architect, at his house on
Krivoarbatsky Lane in Moscow. I had already been in Moscow
a couple of weeks trying to ferret out survivors from the heady days
of the leftist art movement of the early twenties. I had, for example,
a wild-goose chase in search of an old gentleman, once a friend of
Tatlin's, who owned a wing-strut of the glider *Letatlin*. I even tried
to find the man who, as a homeless student of the Vkhutemas
School, had installed himself and his bedding *inside* the
constructivist street monument *The Red Wedge Invades the White
Square*.

One evening, I went to supper with Vavara Rodchenko, the
artist's daughter, in a studio flat that had also been the office of the
magazine *LEF*. The shade of Mayakovsky, one of its editors,
seemed to linger in the room. The bentwood chair you sat on was
Mayakovsky's chair, the plate you ate off was *his* plate, and the fruit
compotier was a present brought from Paris by a man who called
himself 'the cloud in pants'. On the walls there hung a selection of
Rodchenko's paintings—less fine, of course, and less mystical than
those of Malevich, but making up for that with their dazzling display
of vigour. In his daybooks, crammed with sketches, you could
watch him anticipate and race through every style and variation of
the post-war abstract movement in Europe and America. Small
wonder, then, that by 1921 he had believed that easel painting was
dead, and when I asked his daughter whether she still possessed
the three canvases he had shown at the exhibition 'The Last Picture
Has Been Painted', she unrolled on to the floor three square
monochrome canvases: one yellow, one red (and what a red!) and
one blue. For all that, my visit to Mr Melnikov was the high point of
the trip, since, by any standards, the house itself is one of the
architectural wonders of the twentieth century.

The Arbat was once the aristocratic quarter of Moscow. It was
largely rebuilt after the Napoleonic fire in 1812, and even today, in
palaces of green or cream-coloured stucco, one or two of the old
families linger on with their possessions. Melnikov's house—or
rather *pavillon* in the French sense—is set well back from the street,
a building both futurist and classical consisting of two interlocking
cylinders, the rear one taller than the front and pierced with some

Konstantin Melnikov's house.

sixty windows: identical elongated hexagons with constructivist glazing bars. The cylinders are built of brick covered with stucco in the manner of Russian churches. In 1973 the stucco was a dull and flaking ochre, although recent photos show the building spruced up with a coat of whitewash. On the front façade above the architrave are the words KONSTANTIN MELNIKOV ARKHITEKTOR—his proud and lonely boast that true art can only be the creation of the individual, never that of the committee or group.

After I had entered the door on that dark January morning, I climbed the spiral staircase painted emerald green and came into the circular white salon where the architect himself, lying on a kind of Biedermeier *chaise longue*, was having a grated apple for his elevenses. His son, Viktor Stepanovich, was grating the apple. The old man, he explained, could not take much solid food. He was very frail and disillusioned, and when he blinked his hooded eyes one had the sense of hopes abandoned and lost ambitions.

Viktor Stepanovich took me upstairs to the studio that on a summer's day must have been one of the lightest and airiest rooms imaginable, but on this day of muddy clouds and snow flurries the atmosphere was one of liturgical solemnity. He was a painter. His canvases lay this way and that against the walls. He was also something of a mystic and mountain-climber, and while we sat drinking vodka and cracking pine nuts, he showed me several pink Monet-like impressions of dawn in the Caucasus, which struck me as extraordinarily beautiful. When I asked if I could take some photographs of the house, he said, 'You must be quick!' For what I hadn't realized was that Anna Gavrilovna, the architect's wife, was hiding in the bedroom and thoroughly disapproved of having a western visitor.

The house, as I said, was somewhat dilapidated. There were water stains on the walls, and it was not particularly warm. Yet because Melnikov, for reasons of economy as well as aesthetics, had eschewed a slick, mechanical finish, and because he had stuck to the materials of his peasant boyhood—rough-cut planks and plain plaster—the effect was never shoddy but had an air of timeless vitality.

By the time we got downstairs, the old man was sorting through papers on his desk. By the window there was a plaster cast of a Venus: the yearning of a Russian for all things Mediterranean. He showed me photographs and drawings of projects—realized and unrealized—from his entire career.

Among them were the Makhorka Pavilion from the 1925 Moscow Fair; the brilliant free-form arrangement of street stalls at the Sukharevka Market; the Paris Pavilion of 1925; the Paris car-park; the Leyland bus garage in Moscow; his various workers' clubs, which proved that he, like Le Corbusier, was a 'poet' of reinforced concrete; the plan for a monument to Christopher Columbus (to be erected in Santo Domingo); and, finally, a project for the Palace of the Soviets—half pyramid, half lotus—so wild in conception as to make the loonier architectural ramblings of Frank Lloyd Wright seem like so many little sand-castles.

Among the photographs from Paris, he showed me one of himself, a dandified figure standing on the staircase of the Soviet Pavilion. Then, having pointed meticulously to the hatband of his Homburg, his cravat and his spats, he asked me: 'What colour do you think they were?' 'Red,' I suggested. 'Red,' he nodded.

How a private family house—and not any old house but a symbolic coupled duet—came to be built in 1927 in the heart of Moscow, can only be explained within the framework of Melnikov's strange career. Fortunately there is now a first-rate guide in S. Frederick Starr's *Melnikov, Solo Architect in a Mass Society*, from which one can extract the bones of the story. Kostia Melnikov was a bright peasant lad whose father was a milkman. The family home, known as the Hay Lodge, was a cabin sixteen foot square in an outlying suburb of Moscow. 'Today,' he wrote in old age, 'looking back on my works, the source of my individuality is clearly visible . . . in the architecture of that building. Built of clay and straw, it looked like a foreigner in its own homeland . . . but all the magnificent carving of the surrounding houses yielded before it.'

The milkman Melnikov supplied a nearby academy where his young son was soon to be found rooting in the waste-baskets for scraps of paper to draw on. The family apprenticed him to an icon painter. His next job was in a firm of heating engineers whose proprietor, a second-generation Englishman, Vladimir Chaplin, recognized the boy's artistic talents and sent him to the prestigious Moscow School of Painting, Sculpture and Architecture.

This institution, Mayakovsky once said, was the 'only place where they took you without proof of your reliability.' It seems that Chaplin hoped his protégé would blossom into a painter of country scenes and was a bit chagrined when Melnikov changed tack from painting to architecture. The young man, however, was a wonderful architectural draughtsman. He designed schemes for grandiose neoclassical buildings. He married a plump, pretty sixteen-year-old girl from the middle classes, Anna Gavrilovna, and by the time the revolution came he had already built a car factory.

The savage winter of 1917–18 found the young Melnikovs half-starving, back with his family at the Hay Lodge. But gradually, as the nightmare of the civil war receded, Melnikov—like Ladovsky or the Vesnin brothers—began to emerge as one of the most forceful architectural theorists of the renamed Vkhutemas School. His asymmetrical Makhorka Pavilion was a success among intellectuals and workers. At almost no notice, he designed the sarcophagus and glass cover for the embalmed corpse of Lenin and later would recall that one of the Party hacks threatened to have him shot if he didn't get the work done on time. Then in 1925, partly for his proven skill at operating within a minimal budget, he was awarded the commission to build the Soviet Pavilion at the Paris Exposition Internationale des Arts Décoratifs.

With such outstanding exceptions as Le Corbusier's Pavillon de l'Esprit Nouveau, the exhibition was an exercise in opulent kitsch—the essence of art deco. Competing in vulgarity were a pavilion of Old Granada, a Ruhlmann and Patout pavilion, the Italian Fascist-Renaissance pavilion and the English pavilion—perhaps the silliest of all—in the Hollywood-Anglican style.

The Russians, in contrast, with their budget of only 15,000 roubles (at the time the equivalent of 7,650 US dollars), had no alternative but to build light. In fact, the whole structure, which sat on a site between the Grand Palais and the Seine, was made of the cheapest Russian timber, roughly shaped by peasant craftsmen, sent by train from Moscow, erected in next to no time, and painted red, grey and white. Its plan, sliced with two staircases at the diagonal, was incredibly ingenious. Among the exhibits was a small version of Tatlin's tower, which, when the show was over, was left to the French Communist Party, who promptly forgot about it and failed to pay the storage charges of the warehouse, where it sat unrecognized until it was chucked out and probably burned sometime in the early 1960s.

An English publication, put out by His Majesty's Stationery Office, had this to comment: 'The pavilion of Russia was of matchboard construction and was painted red . . . The exterior was largely of glass, and the whole looked like a dilapidated conservatory.' Others compared its aesthetic to that of the guillotine or said it was a 'stab in the back by warriors of the Bolshevik Revolution'. But this did not prevent Melnikov from being the toast of the town, nor the great names of modernism— Hoffmann, Le Corbusier, Perret, Mallet-Stevens—from admitting with great generosity that the Soviets had stolen the show. Le Corbusier took the young Russian under his wing and showed him all the modernist buildings worth seeing—among them his studio for Amedée Ozenfant—which may have put ideas into Melnikov's head about building a place of his own.

Melnikov was even the toast of White Russian *émigrés* who held a costume ball in his honour: guests came dressed as the 'new constructivist architecture'. He went on holiday to Saint-Jean-de-Luz where, in answer to a commission from the Paris city fathers, he devised a scheme for a multi-storey car park for 1,000 cars to be flung across the Seine like a bridge and supported by colossal Atlas-like caryatids on either side. The commission, needless to say, fell through.

Meanwhile, Melnikov's friend Rodchenko, who had come with his project for a workers' reading-room, far from revelling in the high jinks, detested Paris and all it stood for. 'The cult of women,' he wrote home, 'like the cult of worm-infested cheese or oysters, has reached a point where to be fashionable is to be ugly.'

Melnikov, in later years, said he was terribly tempted to stay in France, yet his peasant instincts seem to have called him back. He boarded the train for Moscow, where he soon found he had stirred up a hornet's nest of jealousy in the Vkhutemas School. The denunciations followed, but buoyed up by an apparently limitless faith in his own genius, he decided to press on regardless. He built an extraordinary depot for the Leyland buses which the Soviets had bought from England. Then, in 1927, he set about building his house.

He seems to have hoodwinked Nikolai Bukharin, the party official who put the site at his disposal, that the design would have immediate relevance to the problem of mass public housing. But, as he himself confessed, the time had come, he felt, to be both architect and archi-millionaire.

Given the fertility of his imagination and his litmus-like ability to grasp some feature and use it for his own ends, it is hard, if not impossible, to pin-point Melnikov's sources. He is known, as a student, to have studied the utopian projects of Boullée and Leodoux, both of whom designed cylindrical buildings. He is thought to have admired the interlocking cylinders of grain elevators in the American Midwest, which were published by Le Corbusier in his *L'Esprit Nouveau*. He examined the structure of certain Muscovite churches. And as for the honeycomb construction, whereby windows can be added or subtracted without affecting the weight-load, it reminds me of the cylindrical brick tomb towers of Islamic central Asia. There was, it is well-known, a strong Islamic influence on early Soviet architecture.

I would also like to think that on one of his summer drives around Paris someone drove him to the parish of Chambourcy to see the Desert de Retz, a building that was being 'discovered' around that time by Colette, among others.

The Desert, a colossal truncated doric column with a stack of oval and round rooms piled up around a spiral staircase, was designed and built by an eccentric *anglomane* and friend of Boullée, the Chevalier de Monville. It is surely the most imaginative building of the eighteenth century still standing. Yet, although classed as a national monument since 1941, the French government in its wisdom allowed it to fall into ruin. The windows of the drum are oval and rectangular, but there is something about their arrangement which strikes me as being very close to that of Melnikov's house. At the time I didn't have the wit to ask him, so we shall probably never know.

Melnikov himself—in answer to the self-imposed question: 'What is it that prevents genius from manifesting itself in architecture?'—wrote that his lack of money was converted into an 'immense richness of the imagination'. His sense of autonomy had swept away all sense of caution, and the practical economies forced him to risk as much, relatively speaking, as was risked by Brunelleschi when building the dome of the Florence cathedral.

I never got a chance to go into the bedroom because Anna Gavrilovna was hiding there. I suspect, however, that the altar-like beds had been done away with as well as the uniform yellow-green colour of the walls which Melnikov, who had certain theories about colour and sleeping patterns, associated with restful sleep.

Scattered all over the house were bits of bourgeois furniture, neoclassical chairs or an art nouveau carpet—in fact, throughout there was an atmosphere of antimacassar and samovar at odds with the original spirit. Viktor Stepanovich told me that during the years of the Stalinist 'night' his mother had salvaged whatever she could from her old family home.

Melnikov, mercifully, did not have to share the fate—of cattle-trucks to Siberia—which befell a Mandelstam, a Babel or a Meyerhold. Yet gradually the vultures closed in. First his colleagues denounced him as a formalist. Then at a meeting of the Soviet architectural establishment about 800 hands shot up in support of a motion that would prevent him from practising his profession.

The death-knell of visionary architecture in Russia had already been sounded when Lenin's commissioner for enlightenment, Anatoly Lunacharsky, announced, 'The people also have a right to colonnades.' It did, admittedly, take time for the spread of that deadly megalomaniac style known as Sovnovrok (New Soviet Rococo), which was bound to be anathema to Melnikov. For forty years he simply sat at home doing nothing. From time to time there was talk of his rehabilitation, but nothing really came of it, so that by the time of my visit the house, for all its vestiges of vitality, had become a sombre and gloomy private palace—as sombre as Prokofiev's 1942 Sonata.

When I bade the old man goodbye, he smiled a smile of wistful melancholy and, raising one hand, drew in the air a graph of his blighted career. If one could have recorded it accurately on paper, it might have looked something like this:

COLIN THUBRON
THE OLD
SILK ROUTE

The trees were neither living nor dead: a Grimm forest of willows convulsed by vanished winds. Their roots sank so deep that they found moisture which never reached the surface, but the thinning sap had desiccated their leaves, and their bark had loosened and split. Behind them a grey piedmont gravel, pushed down from the Tianshan snows, was smeared across hundreds of square miles of sand. In front, the true desert began.

Our spirits rose, as if the weight of eastern China, which lay far behind us, was suddenly lifted. For a moment, I think, my companions too wanted to be alone. As for me, solitude seemed the natural condition of travel. Alone, I was at once more vulnerable and more sensitized, and even China appeared no longer precisely a strange land. I was just a stranger in it, my identity thinned. And this solitude carried an inner excitement, which has been perfectly distinct to me since childhood.

But now the company of my own people—a television camera team—filled me with misgiving. In a film, the lone traveller's windfalls—the chance intimacies and impulses—are gone. Solitude can only be recreated. Yet our film aimed to record the Chinese Silk Road through my eyes, and I nursed a fantasy that our journey would somehow bifurcate. I would experience it, and they would shoot it. The two processes could be decently separated, just as the writing of a travel book is separate from the journey it records.

Such a daydream must have belonged to a time of innocence twenty-five years before, when I made freelance documentaries alone, wandering about Morocco and Japan with a cine-camera and a tape-recorder slung over my back. The films' ideas, script, shooting had all been mine, and their technical naïvety had been balanced, I suppose, by some raw freshness.

But now I was only the visual tip of a corporate iceberg. Behind me trudged a two-man camera crew, a sound-recordist, the director, his assistant, a Mandarin interpreter, a Turkic interpreter, two camel-drivers and seven camels loaded with cameras, tripods and stock-boxes.

Yet for the screen we were fabricating solitude.

We journeyed in the unnatural silence of huge beasts treading in softness. The wind had dropped to nothing. The camels' hooves left dim circles in the powdery earth. Once or twice we crossed the

129

tracks of intermittent rivers, now dry. Their starved reeds splintered at our touch; our feet crunched through their beds. Then the forest gave way to stunted red willows until even these had reverted to dust—ancient-looking mounds of roots and crumbled wood littered over the sand.

If I had charted the most landlocked spot on earth, the arms of my compass would have intersected here, in China's far northwest. Its heart is a howling wilderness, 600 miles wide, where the winds have buried and mummified whole caravans. The native Uighurs call it Taklimakan, 'You enter and you never return.' Aurel Stein thought Arabia tame by comparison. Sven Hedin called it the world's most dangerous desert. Its dunes rise to 300 feet, and in sudden temperature changes the moving sands make hallucinatory noises, as if caravans or troupes of musicians were passing nearby. So at night, wrote Marco Polo, 'the stray traveller will hear as it were the tramp and hum of a great cavalcade of people away from the real line of march, and taking this to be their own company they will follow the sound; and when day breaks they find that a cheat has been put on them and that they are in an ill plight. Even in daytime one hears those spirits talking . . .'

But I could hear nobody talking, except my own countrymen— shared gossip, jokes, assumptions. We sheltered in our own culture. We plodded across the sand in disparate groups, complaining about Chinese bureaucracy and the cameleers. Nobody else seemed to be missing a lonely fraternization with the land. Perhaps, I thought, the habit of living alone had paradoxically exacerbated my awareness of people: until their presence obliterated everything else. But it seemed now that this companionship enfolded us all in a balloon of Britishness: amiable, safe, uncreative.

We intruded on the desert like a regiment. Only in the lens were some of us—three select camels, my guide and I—effortlessly, romantically isolated. We five moved in the borrowed glory of Lawrence and Doughty. Even my guide, in his flat cap and loose trousers, was touched by a shambling glamour. As we went, the horizon was closed by shallow hills stubbled with tamarisk, and in front of us range upon range of stark dunes came beating in out of emptiness. The land was simplifying itself, shedding its stones first,

then its trees, then its shrubs. Horses were useless in this terrain—
their hooves burned in the sand—and donkeys slowly weakened.
Only the twin-humped Bactrian camel, which can go waterless for
two weeks, travelled the wastes at all. Its long, slender legs lift its
body as if on stilts above the surface heat, and its spatular feet
dissipate the impact of its tread. It only starts to sweat—mildly—in
a temperature at which a man would be dead.

I watched these three sauntering in train behind us. They
carried plastic water-containers, bedding, tent-poles, food-boxes.
(They carried film equipment too, but it was concealed under a
native rug.) They were like emissaries of the desert's strangeness.
Their rhythmic swaying echoed the surge of its dunes. Shaggy
fringes dribbled down the underside of their necks like inverted
manes, and each head rose to a punkish tuft far back on the
forehead, above long-lashed eyes and vain lips. They shared an air
of randy contempt.

Before us the desert wrinkled to the horizon in a tumult of
ghostly curves. The deepening silence, the intensifying heat, the
ever-purer slopes, suggested that we were approaching some
presence—or primal absence—in the wastes. Was this, the viewer
might have wondered, a paradigm of the ultimate journey, the
paring away of everything essential, little by little, as we advanced
into the heart of Nothing?

But no. We were conscious mainly of mild boredom and an
unheroic thirst (we had plenty of water). Our glamour rested only
in the eyes of others. It is uncertain if we were really journeying at
all. We were creating the likeness of a journey.

In fact, we were undergoing not one voyage, but two. The first of
these was real but stayed unfilmed—the director's battle for
transport and locations, the crew's struggling with light and
angles; whereas the second—the imaginary journey which it
produced—was a celluloid narrative of premeditated images, the
voyage whose destination was always known (since everything had
to be prepared in advance), fostered in an illusion of naturalness by
camera-shots repeated over and over. This was the ghost-journey,
in which I was an actor. It was produced only for the screen.

So I became nostalgic for writing. A travel-book is an account:

131

it records the real. A travel-film is an illusion: it reconstructs it. And the confusion of this harassed both the director and me. He was an austerely sensitive man, who instinctively wanted to mould the film to a travel-writer's energies. But travelling like this, I could only imagine those energies. I could not feel them. So while he tried to envisage our journey through the eyes of a writer, I perversely began to see it through the lens of a film director.

But this was obscured by more brutal confusions. We were at the mercy of four Uighurs, local Turkomen more volatile than the native Chinese, who dwindle to a minority in this far north-west. The Uighur had once made the Silk Road work: opportunists trading between the static hierarchies of China and the empires to the west. But as far as our film was concerned, only one Uighur (my guide) existed. The other three—two camel herdsmen and an interpreter—accompanied us invisibly: part of the true journey which lurked beneath the film. They belonged to the chaos of real travel. They split into factions. The guide and interpreter came from one village, the cameleers from another. They wrangled, and fell into bitter silences.

The camels, too, were not what they seemed. They had been assembled in advance from different regions of the province, but were less beasts of burden than herd animals. They bellowed resentment at their loads, and suddenly broke loose and rampaged over the desert, scattering boxes and blankets in their wake. It was a star performance. But we could not film it: because our cameras were on their backs. The cameleers followed them, mutinously. And all afternoon we marched on south, looking for sand unblemished by any speck of scrub, ranges which would say to the camera: this is the harshest desert on earth.

The camera, after its fashion, was demanding truth.

At last, by evening, we arrived. Long, virgin dunes curved photogenically in front of us, and the camels were back in harness. We had reconvened the mythic elements of our journey. The three most filmic beasts, their loads reassembled for continuity, paraded along the dune-lips behind the guide and me. But we were, of course, going nowhere in particular. We were completing patterns of backlit beauty for the lens, creating compositions, lending proportion and drama. The director and camera crew, squatting like guerrillas on strategic hillocks, directed our passage through walkie-talkies. We gazed hypocritically through them into solitude. The four camels which did not officially exist coughed unseen in a dip of the sands. How did we look?

The cameraman worried about the slant of evening light. The dunes, he said, were pointing the wrong way. The director pondered and shuffled unsurely. Wherever the lens swung, there was cliché: skyline, camel-train, sunset, us. We were trapped in other people's daydreams.

I tried to imagine how we appeared. Compared to our surroundings, I felt, we must look weirdly insubstantial. Again I was reminded of ghosts, trying pathetically to integrate with the real. Perhaps the paranoia of Hollywood directors, I thought, was due to the terrifying precariousness of their control. A film seemed to belong to nobody. It was in the hands not only of financiers and the elements, but of cameramen and actors (myself now) and of the sheer recalcitrance of images, which never reproduced themselves predictably. And in the end, for all the arts of editing and commentary, the lens would give back to the viewer his own vision: he would see simply what he would have seen if he were standing where the camera stood.

By comparison, my trade as a writer seemed megalomaniac. I was the lens, even the viewer. Everything I wrote was subjective.

Then reality broke in. As the guide and I ascended too steep a slope, the camels floundered to their knees. They collapsed in sequence, like cards. Their leading-ropes broke. They struggled and roared. I tried to beat the hindmost to its feet, but the baggage was slipping over its humps. Its buried legs gained no purchase in the sand. Its slobbering face sank level with mine. I struck its flank several times before I noticed it was defecating—a piece of cruelty faithfully recorded by the cameras on the far dune. For minutes the sand writhed and slithered away under us, as if we were treading water. And even after we had painfully reassembled on the dune's crest, the reputation of camels was confirmed. The lead beast flailed out and lacerated my guide's shin.

I felt suddenly guilty. It was as if a fictional character had lunged out of our film, and kicked. All at once I imagined the film eating up everyone around it. Except me. I was its supposed hero, already incarnate in it. Yet I was accompanied by people who had traversed precisely the same land as I had, and who would appear on screen only as names at the end.

At dusk we put up a makeshift wind-break. Our camp-fire blazed and subsided, while an invisible haze, reaching far up the horizon, obliterated the stars. Since we had to rise for the dawn light, the camels were fed in darkness, and for hours I was kept awake by the crash of their teeth into piles of brittle foliage, and watched their profiles as they shambled back and forth between the fodder and a futile search for plants. Sometimes they would squeak in a peculiar, unofficial way, as if in distress; and one great beast, passing the shelter where we lay, sank its fangs into the newly cut tent-poles and brought them crashing on to our heads before it trotted contemptuously into the night.

The unfilmed moment touched us only with dazed ill temper. It belonged merely to life. There was no light by which to film it and besides, the journey was not meant to be happening to the others, only to me.

But next morning, the dawn shone perfect. The most docile beasts fell into line behind me with their baggage and continuity intact. The backlit dunes were pronounced correct, and rippled accommodatingly. And I stepped again into the legend of a real journey—a voyage through random light and circumstance, to an unknown horizon, alone.

NORMAN LEWIS
SIAM

Thailand, until 1953 generally called Siam, went modern just before my first visit there, later in that year. Marshal Pibul Songkhram, the ruling autocrat, ordered the nation to cease to look to the past, and to take the future in a firm embrace. A commission sent to the US to investigate western culture returned with its findings. Its members believed that it was rooted in whisky drinking, dancing in public and the strip-tease, and urged the introduction of these customs into Siam. It was at first stipulated that the strip-tease should be performed under religious auspices in the precincts of a temple—although this provision soon went by the board.

Hat Yai, a provincial town in the south within a few miles of the Malaysian frontier, was chosen for an experiment in instant modernization, and I went there to see what was happening. There was a tendency in Siam for the words 'modern' and 'American' to be used interchangeably, so when the order went out for Hat Yai to be brought up to date, most Thais accepted that it was to be Americanized. Little surprise was aroused when the model chosen for the new Hat Yai was Dodge City of the 1860s as revealed by the movies.

In due course the experts arrived with photographs of the capital of the wild frontier in its heyday, and within weeks the comfortable muddle of Hat Yai was no more. Its shacks reeling on their stilts were pulled down, the ducks and buffaloes chased out of the ditches, and the spirit houses (after proper apologies to the spirits) shoved out of sight. It became illegal to fly kites within the limits of the town, or to stage contests between fighting fish.

Where the bustling chaos of the East had once been, arose a replica of the main street made famous by so many westerns, complete with swing-door saloons, wall-eyed hotels and the rickety verandas on which law-abiding citizens had been marshalled by the sheriff to go on a posse, and men of evil intention planned their attack on the mail-train or the bank. Hat Yai possessed no horses and the hard men of those days rode into town in Jeeps—nevertheless hitching-posts were provided. For all the masquerade, Hat Yai in the 1950s did bear some slight resemblance to the Dodge City of a century before, and there were gun-fighters in plenty in the vicinity. It was at that time an unofficial rest-area for Malaysian

137

communist guerrillas from across the frontier, tolerated simply because the Thais lacked the strength to keep them out. The communist intruders were armed to the teeth, and Thai law-enforcement agents—part of whose uniform included Davy Crockett fur caps from which racoons' tails dangled—were few in number. Reaching for one's gun was a matter of frequent occurrence in the main-street saloons. Although it was largely a histrionic gesture and few people were shot, newcomers like myself were proudly taken to be shown the holes in the ceilings.

The arrival of the movies played their part in Pibul Songkhram's vision of the new Thailand. In a single year, 1950, hundreds, perhaps thousands of movie-theatres opened up all over south-east Asia, the first film on general release being *Arsenic and Old Lace*. With this the shadow play that had entertained so many generations of Thais was wiped out overnight. A multitude of mothers throughout the land had worked tirelessly at pressing back their daughters' fingers from the age of five to enable them to dance with style in dramas such as the *Ramayana*. From this point on it was all to no purpose, and the customers who befuddled themselves in the saloons with Mekong whisky, drunk hot by the half-pint, were waited upon with sublime grace by girls whose days as performers were at an end. Real-life theatre demanded the imaginative effort of suspending belief; cowboy movies did not.

Investigating the threatened disappearance of the puppet-show, a Bangkok newspaper reported that it had only been able to discover a single company surviving somewhere in the north of the country, working in Thai style with life-size puppets manipulated not by strings, but by sticks from below stage. It took forty years to train a puppeteer to the required pitch of perfection in this art, and it seemed worthwhile to the newspaper to bring this company down to Bangkok to film what was likely to be one of its last performances.

This was given in the garden of the paper's editor, Kukrit Pramoj, and attracted a fashionable crowd of upper-crust Thais, plus a few foreign diplomats, many of whom would see a puppet-show for the first and last time. So unearthly was the skill of the puppeteers, so naturalistic and convincing the movements of the puppets, that, but for the fact that their vivacity surpassed that of flesh and blood, it would have been tempting to suspect we were watching actors in puppet disguise.

After the show most of the guests went off to a smart restaurant, filling it with the bright clatter of enthusiasm that would soon fade. Such places provided 'continental' food—the mode of the day. In this land offering so many often extraordinary regional delicacies, successful efforts were made to suppress flavour to a point that only a saporific vacuum remained. Kukrit, always a champion of Thai culture, made the astonishing admission that he knew nothing of the cuisine, now only to be savoured at night markets and roadside stalls. In a flare-up of nationalist enthusiasm, he announced his determination to put this right. He made inquiries among his friends and a few days later I received an invitation to lunch with him at the house of a relation, a prince who was a grandson of King Chulalongkorn. The prince, said Kukrit, employed a chef trained to cook nothing but European food, and he could not remember whether—if ever—he had tasted a local dish. Entering into the spirit of adventure, he had been able to track down a Thai cook with an enthusiastic following in the half-world of the markets, who would be hired for this occasion. The meal thus, for him too, offered the promise of novelty and adventure.

The prince lived on the outskirts of Bangkok in a large villa dating from about 1900. It was strikingly English in appearance, with a garden full of sweet peas, grown by the prince himself, which in this climate produced lax, greyish blooms, singularly devoid of scent. He awaited us at the garden gate. Kukrit leaped down from the car, scrambled towards him and despite Songkhram's injunction to refrain from salutations of a servile kind, made a token grab at his right ankle. This the prince good-naturedly avoided. 'Do get up, Kukrit dear boy,' he said. Both men had been to school in England, and, as well as their easy, accent-free mastery of the language, there was something that proclaimed this in their faces and manner.

My previous experience of Thai houses had been limited to the claustrophobic homes in which the moneyed classes had taken refuge, shuttered away from the menacing light of day in a gloom deepened by a clutter of dark furniture. The villa came as a surprise, for in the past year an avant-garde French interior designer had flown in to bring about a revolution. He had brought the sun back, filtering it through lattices and the dappled shade of house-plants with great, lustrous leaves, opening the house to light and diffusing an ambience of spring. This was from the womb of the future. We lunched under a photo-mural of Paris—*quand fleurit le printemps*—and a device invented by the designer breathed a faint fragrance of narcissi through the conditioned air. The meal was both delicious and enigmatic, based, we were assured, on the choice of the correct basic materials (none of them identified), and colours that were auspicious given the phase of the moon. Kukrit took many notes.

The entertainment that followed was in some ways more singular, for the prince told us that he had inherited most of his grandfather's photographic equipment, including his stereoscopic slides, and he proposed that we should view them together—'to give you some idea of how royalty lived in those days.'

King Chulalongkorn, who reigned from 1868 to 1910, was a man of protean achievement. On the world stage he showed himself more than a match for the French colonial power that entertained barely concealed hopes of gobbling up his kingdom. At home he pursued many hobbies with unquenchable zest; organizing fancy-dress parties, cooking for his friends, but above all immersing himself in his photography. He collected cameras by the hundred, did his own developing, and drew upon an immense family pool of consorts and their children for his portraiture. We inspected photographs, taken at frequent intervals, of his sons lined up, ten at a time in order of height, for the king's loving record of their advance from childhood to adolescence, all of them, including the six-year-old at the bottom of the line, in a top hat. Toppers had only been put aside in one case when four senior sons had been crammed into the basket of a balloon.

The queens and consorts were of even more interest, and here they were seen posed in the standard environment of Victorian studio photography; lounging against plaster Greek columns, taking a pretended swipe with a tennis racquet, or clutching the handlebars of a weird old bicycle. Fancy-dress shots, of which there were many, bore labels in French, the language of culture of the day: *L'Amazone* (Queen Somdej with a feather in her hair grasping a bow); *Une Dame Turque de qualité* (the Princess of Chiang Mai, with a hookah); *La Cavalerie Legère* (an unidentified consort in a hussar's shako); *La Jolie Chochère* (another consort, in white breeches and a straw hat, carrying a whip). The impression given by this collection was that the Victorian epoch produced a face of its own, and that this could even triumph over barriers of race. Thus Phra Rataya, Princess of Chiang Mai, bore a resemblance to George Sand; Queen Somdej had something about her of La Duse, while a lesser consort, well into middle age, reminded me of one of my old Welsh aunts.

The prince put away the slides. Like his grandfather King Chulalongkorn, and his great-grandfather, King Mongkut— an astronomer and inventor who designed a quick-firing cannon based on the Colt revolver—he had a taste for intellectual pleasures. He showed us his Leica camera with its battery of lenses. Candid photography was in vogue at the time. By use of gadgets such as angle-view finders it was possible to catch subjects for portraiture off-guard, sometimes in ludicrous postures. There was no camera to equal it for this purpose, said the prince. As for his grandfather's gear, it took up rather a lot of space, and he said he would be quite happy to donate it to any museum that felt like giving it house-room.

As we strolled together across the polished entrance hall towards the door, my attention was suddenly taken by what appeared to be a large, old-fashioned and over-ornate birdcage suspended in an environment in which nothing was more than a year old. I stopped to examine it, and the prince said, 'Uncle lives there.'

Although slightly surprised, I thought I understood. 'You mean the house spirit?'

'Exactly. In this life he was our head servant. He played an important part in bringing up us children, and was much loved by us all. Uncle was quite ready to sacrifice himself for the good of the family.'

The prince had no hesitation in explaining how this had come about. When the building of a new royal house was finished, a bargain might be struck with a man of low caste. The deal was that he would agree to surrendering the remaining few years of the present existence in return for acceptance into the royal family in the next. He would be entitled to receive ritual offerings on a par with the ancestors. Almost without exception, such an arrangement was readily agreed to.

'How did uncle die?'

The prince answered enigmatically: 'He was interred under the threshold. Being still a child I was excluded from the ceremony, which was largely a religious one. Everyone was happy. Certainly uncle was.'

I took the risk. 'Would a western education have any effect at all on such beliefs?' I asked.

'That is a hard question,' the Prince said, 'but I am inclined to the opinion that it would be slight. This appears to be more a matter of feeling than conscious belief. Education is an imperfect shield against custom and tradition.' We stood together in the doorway and the cage swayed a little in a gust of warm breeze. 'In some ways,' the prince said, 'you may judge us still to be a little backward.' His laugh seemed apologetic. 'In others I hope you will agree that we move with the times.'

IAN BURUMA
TAIWAN

The young colonel pointed through the window at the coast of China: 'There it is, the mainland, bandit territory,' he said, using the official jargon not much heard these days outside military circles. 'And on your left, you see Kin-men.' You could see most of the island, better known as Quemoy, with its neat paddy-fields and mud-coloured villages. Like most front lines against communism, Quemoy, the small island between mainland China and nationalist Taiwan, is a little absurd. The last major battle there was in 1958. Since then there have been exchanges of pot-shots, but those ended in the late 1970s. Yet there are guards at every intersection—one always wearing a gas-mask. On the beaches there are anti-landing devices and barbed-wire fencing; the waters are said to be mined. There is a field hospital dug deep into the granite rock, part of a network of underground tunnels spanning the whole island. It is extremely expensive and almost entirely symbolic, for the struggle itself is symbolic, waged mostly by the Political Warfare Department.

In the Political Warfare Museum the visitor is shown photographs of poor mainland Chinese peasants, toiling *en masse*, like Egyptian slaves in a Cecil B. De Mille epic. There are pictures of atrocities committed during the Cultural Revolution. There are everyday items: old tubes of toothpaste; dusty, rock-hard bars of soap; torn and stained clothes. In contrast there is Taiwan: photos of laughing people at the seaside and nice new apartment buildings, samples of attractive tinned foods, colourful T-shirts, pop-music cassettes and miniature video games—all of which are packed into helium balloons, or plastic floats, and dispatched to the mainland as examples of modern prosperity and benevolent rule—proof that the Kuomintang, the ruling party of the Republic of China, takes better care of its people than the Communist Party. 'It is very important that the people on the mainland know this,' said the colonel, 'for then they will be on our side.'

And the nationalist Kuomintang is everywhere, a benevolent Big Brother—in Confucian terms, Superior Man—whose legitimacy lies in his capacity to take care of little people. In Taiwan, the Superior Men are the élite from mainland China, ruling the Taiwanese people, trying to shape them in their own mainland

image. This image is inescapable. The National Palace Museum; the memorials, statues and portraits of the two nationalist leaders, Generalissimo Chiang Kai-shek and Sun Yat-sen, the promulgation of Chiang Kai-shek's writings and perhaps more important, Sun Yat-sen's Three Principles of the People: Nationalism, Democracy and Prosperity. The image is conveyed in the national language, Mandarin Chinese, brought over by Chiang Kai-shek's mainlanders in 1949—the official language on an island where almost eighty per cent of the population speaks the Fukien dialect, about as different from Mandarin as Italian from French.

The National Palace Museum itself is not just a museum with the finest collection of classical Chinese art in the world, but a symbol of the official national identity. Chin Hsiao-yi, the director of the museum, used to be private secretary to Chiang Kai-shek. He is a senior member of the Kuomintang Central Committee, and was one of the most powerful men in Taiwan.

When we met in a large reception room, there were professors, curators and various secretaries in stiff-backed Chinese chairs to take notes and tend tape-recorders. Chin was explaining how the museum demonstrated 5,000 years of 'cultural homogeneity and continuity'.

Would he ever consider showing modern art in the museum; that is, art produced after the Chinese empire came to an end in 1911?

Yes, indeed, there was now a gallery devoted to modern Chinese art. Unfortunately, however, 'much modern art is so influenced by the West that it is cut off from the great Chinese tradition. Those works cannot be shown in the museum.'

How long can the pretence that Taiwan represents *all* of China be sustained? Recovering the mainland has been the principal theme of Kuomintang propaganda.

'What would we be without the aim of recovering the mainland?' asked a government official. 'With an independent republic, what would we be? Who knows about Taiwan? People confuse it with Thailand.'

Taiwan and China may share a cultural heritage but since 1949 Taiwan has come into its own, not just as another Chinatown, but

TAIWAN

NORTH KOREA

SOUTH KOREA

CHINA

JAPAN

SHANGHAI ●

EAST CHINA SEA

FUKIEN
PROVINCE

TAIPEI
●

KIN-MEN
(QUEMOY)

TAIWAN

◁ Lan Yü

as a modern nation albeit without official independence. That is: how can Taiwan, a modern Chinese state, identify itself with Chinese civilization if it is not 'China'? The temporary answer is to assert that it is.

I was shown a promotional film at the Government Information Office in Taipei. It made the usual points about preserving the 5,000-year heritage, the benevolent rule under the Three Principles and Taiwan's remarkable prosperity. The points were not invalid. But the film was disingenuous: 'After the heroic struggle against the Japanese warlords,' as the film's narrator put it, the Generalissimo and his loyalists found Taiwan to be a 'backward, undeveloped agricultural society . . . a blank slate, ideal for carrying out reconstruction based upon the Three Principles . . . We started with nothing and ended with an economic miracle.' This is what children learn at school. Taiwan was a blank slate. The Chinese *mission civilisatrice* began in 1949. As a result, the Taiwanese descendants of the 'early-comers' (as the officials like to call them—mainlanders are 'late-comers') are taught to remember a history they never had.

Modern Taiwanese history began in 1895, when China ceded Formosa to Japan. Formosans wishing to remain Chinese were allowed to register as such and leave for the mainland. Those remaining became citizens of the Japanese Empire in 1898. Formosa was to become a show-case of superior Japanese colonialism, of Tokyo's Manifest Destiny. The Japanese wanted to shape the colony in *their* own image. 'Un-Japanese' behaviour was punished. Elderly people were lectured for wearing Chinese jackets and trousers. Their Chinese-style buttons were sometimes ripped off. Traditional architecture, food and housing arrangements were criticized as un-Japanese, thus uncivilized. Shinto shrines were built all over the island, and Chinese household gods were replaced by Shinto symbols. The Japanese language was taught at schools. Everything was Japanized: Confucian ethics were presented in schools as Japanese ideals or, like the Three Principles, as universal ideals, shared by the Chinese.

Modernization was forced through with a ruthless efficiency. The statistics were impressive. In 1931, Taiwan had 2,857 miles of public and private railroad track; the whole of mainland China had fewer than 9,400 miles. Radio-telephone communication between Tokyo and Taipei was opened in 1934. Telegraph and postal services served every town and many villages. The power-stations generated almost as much electricity as the total produced in the whole of China. Taiwan's first university, now called Taiwan National University, was set up by the Japanese in 1927.

Japanese culture is now everywhere, frequently in a western guise—its origins blurred, suppressed or forgotten. For instance, Taipei, one of the great *nouveau riche* cities of east Asia. In the first quarter of the century, the city was rebuilt by the Japanese in the image of a European-style colonial capital. Many of the broad avenues, neat public parks and pompous public buildings remain. Nationalists with more zeal than taste constantly talk of pulling them down. 'They are bad buildings,' said one government official in Taipei, 'they are not Chinese.'

After the war, the city was transformed once more, this time into the temporary capital of the Republic of China. Today, the economic boom, influenced by America and following the example of Japan, has changed the capital yet again. And the concrete dust has not yet settled. Colourful billboards show glimpses of the future: high-rise flats, elevated highways and, an essential touch this, a small Chinese garden or pagoda in the foreground. Until then, Taipei remains brash, lively and in dubious taste. American fast food, Japanese TV culture and Fukienese folklore feed a hunger for colour and kitsch. Kitsch is endemic to Taiwan, as almost every image is displaced, borrowed from elsewhere. Popular culture coexists uneasily with the high Chinese traditions imported from the mainland in 1949 and officially imposed on Taiwan to give the former Japanese colony a new Chinese identity. It has lent the place a schizophrenic quality.

The surface of modern Taiwan looks familiar to anyone who knows Japan. The coffee-shops, with their quasi-baroque, partly French-château, partly alpine-Swiss interiors, where teenage girls eat spaghetti and chocolate parfaits. The sing-along *karaoke* bars, where customers sing Japanese songs through microphones, accompanied by taped background music and video pictures of lonely Japanese women in evening dresses staring romantically at the harbour lights of Yokohama. The TV variety shows, with their endless parade of mediocre teenage singers performing in clouds of dry ice. Like the colonial buildings, they are Japanese fantasies of Europe and America transferred to Taiwan: forms of modern kitsch twice removed from their source. What to call it? Japanese modern? Asian baroque?

2

For ten years Antonio Chiang edited a magazine, *The Eighties*, that was opposed to the Kuomintang government and published by Kang Ning-hsiang, one of the most prominent opposition politicians. *The Eighties* was often banned, but somehow Chiang always managed to stay out of jail and keep his magazine in print. Chiang is the kind of intellectual that radical idealists like to hate; in revolutionary terms, a Danton as opposed to a Robespierre. He takes pride in being Taiwanese, but is too cosmopolitan, too sophisticated, too well-read to be comfortable in the narrow world of Taiwanese nationalism. Indeed, he is somewhat contemptuous of it. His new magazine, *The Journalist*, attempts to stay away from opposition politics altogether. Although he has a wide following among the Taiwanese, and his views are constantly sought by foreigners, he cuts a somewhat sad figure. He, more than anyone else I met in Taiwan, exemplified the man trapped between worlds. Cut off from China, and too Chinese (or Taiwanese) to choose a life of comfortable obscurity in America, Chiang is confined to the insularity of Taiwan.

He invited me to a friend's house in Beitou, a hot-spring resort near Taipei. The house, built by the owner, a well-known Taiwanese artist sympathetic to the opposition, had a large communal bath, Japanese-style (the Chinese prefer to take baths in private). We slipped into the scalding water which smelled of rotten eggs. I asked Chiang whether forty years of Kuomintang education had worked. Were young Taiwanese losing their Taiwaneseness, were they really identifying with the official image of mainland China?

No, he said, it had not worked. 'Inside Taiwan we see ourselves

as Chinese, but as soon as we step off the island, we are Taiwanese.'

It was a typically Taiwanese answer. I had asked a Taiwanese girl in a disco the same question. She wanted to leave to live in America. 'This place is too small, too narrow. But I was born as a Taiwanese, so I will always have a home. Mainlanders are different . . . they don't care about this place. It is not their home.' One of her friends, a mainlander, giggled: 'Don't listen to her, she is prejudiced.'

At a lunch organized by the Government Information Office, I sat next to an elegant lady just back from Paris. She wore an expensive fur coat and talked incessantly about 'creativity'. She worked in the theatre. 'We are so free here,' she said, bubbling over in excitement, 'we can do anything we like.' She was a mainlander.

I asked her whether the complicated relationship between mainlanders and Taiwanese was too sensitive a subject for drama or literature.

Not at all, she answered, but it is simply not an issue here. 'Nobody even thinks about it.'

'Well,' said a government bureaucrat, in the smiling manner of a tactful host trying to ease his guests on to another subject, 'we Chinese all have regional feelings, Taiwan is no exception. But it is not an issue anyway.' He conceded that thirty years ago it might have been a problem, but with young people today, 'it is not an issue.'

I pressed the point again, which was rude. Chinese banquets are like diplomatic functions: occasions for polite small-talk. Were there any plays or books about prejudice or discrimination among Taiwanese and mainlanders?

No, said both the lady and the bureaucrat, 'it is not an issue.'

Another official, who had been listening with an air of irritation, broke into the conversation. His face was red with anger. He was half-Taiwanese, half-mainlander, he said, and thoroughly sick of talking to foreigners about the subject. 'Only foreign journalists are interested in it,' he said. He was starting to shout. 'Sure, it is a good story. But here only a minority is conscious of it. It is purely political.'

The artistic lady agreed. 'Politicians are always looking for controversy, it is more fun.' She giggled.

But is it too sensitive a subject for the theatre?

The man was now shaking with rage. 'Yes, it is political and very sensitive and I would certainly not want any books or plays on this issue.'

It is sensitive because it reveals an elementary truth about Taiwanese society. The Kuomintang party does not consist only of nationalist Chinese from the mainland. Indeed, now, most members of the Kuomintang were born in Taiwan itself. The opposition, however, consists almost exclusively of Taiwanese: it is more than a struggle against authoritarian rule. It is a matter of identity.

3

Both the Japanese and the Kuomintang party tried either to subordinate or destroy the Taiwanese élite. One of the most painful events in post-war Taiwan, carefully deleted from the public memory, was the massacre of Taiwanese on 28 April 1947 by nationalist troops commanded by Ch'en Yi, a notorious governor of Fukien during the war. The Taiwanese élite, having struggled so long for home rule under the Japanese, resented the way the island was taken over and plundered by the nationalist regime on the mainland. Resentment boiled over into rebellion, nationalist troops were shipped in and thousands—some say tens of thousands—of Taiwanese civilians were killed. The message was clear to generations of Taiwanese: politics is dangerous; it is safer to get rich. The 28 April massacre became a taboo subject. It is not taught at school, and many parents prefer not to tell their children.

Hong Chi-chang, a prominent member of the opposition party, the DPP, wants to revive the memory. He hopes to make 28 April a national day of reconciliation. The government is asked formally to apologize for the massacre. Hong's '28 April Movement' also wishes the government to abolish the 'place of origin' requirement on identity cards. 'Taiwanese,' he says, 'must be identified by residency, not family background.' The aim is an independent Taiwan, a Taiwan for the Taiwanese; a new élite has grown up to challenge the old one which clings to its hope of recovering the mainland. And a hopeless dream is no match for provincial nationalism.

In Taipei I went to see a new film about aboriginal girls sold as prostitutes to the shabby low-class brothels of Huahsi, an area of Taipei known to tourists as Snake Alley. It was not a good film, at once sensational, titillating and sentimental. I saw the film with an aboriginal couple, Mr and Mrs Chen. I felt embarrassed for them and assumed that they had hated it. I was wrong. Mr Chen liked it. He liked it because it was about 'his people'.

Mr Chen is a civil servant. He belongs to the Tayal tribe from central Taiwan described in the 1920s by Harry A. Franck as 'the fiercest, the most persistent, and the most successful head-hunters.' Today most of the aboriginal prostitutes in Snake Alley are Tayal. Mr Chen was one of the few aboriginals with a university degree. After studying in America for several years, he worked as a journalist in central Taiwan. But he was hindered in his work because he spoke little Taiwanese, only the official Mandarin Chinese. The Taiwanese would not trust Mr Chen, so he had trouble getting stories. He decided to join the government.

I asked him what he said when people in America inquired about his nationality.

'Of course Chinese.'

But did he feel Chinese?

'My tribal identity is still very strong. But I feel honoured to be part of the Chinese family. We were taught about the great Chinese civilization. I would like to visit China one day. Even so, some people don't respect us. They think we are barbarians.'

Which people?

'Difficult to say. Well, the Taiwanese. They call themselves native Taiwanese, but they are not. We are. If they would take over our government, I don't know how we would be treated.' He said he believed in the aim of recovering the mainland, because he did not want to stay on the island: 'I have a global vision.'

It is a common pattern: the oppressed minority identifies with the ruling outsiders to keep the oppressive majority at a distance. It was the story of the *montagnards* in Indo-China, who first helped the French and then the Americans against the Vietnamese. The

154

Ambonese did the same for the Dutch during their rule in the Dutch East Indies. And it was the story of the Taiwanese tribes under the Japanese, despite some violent uprisings and bloody massacres.

Mr Chen's father could remember the bloodiest rebellion, in 1930, in Wushe in central Taiwan. He now owns a hot-spring hotel in the mountains near the same place and plants tea on the mountain slopes. He calls his children by their Japanese names. We visited his old village, still populated by aboriginals. The village was a few narrow streets with wooden shacks. The only modern buildings were a Presbyterian and a Catholic church. A loudspeaker from the Presbyterian church urged people to send their children to Sunday school. The announcement was made in Mandarin and in the tribal language. There are 320,000 aborigines in Taiwan. Seventy thousand are members of the Presbyterian church. There is a similar number of Catholics. Most were converted after the war. A young aboriginal social worker called Ziro said that 'Christianity stopped us from being head-hunters. It didn't force us, like the Japanese did, but it gave us a moral brake.'

A Canadian missionary called Michael took me to Lan Yü, or Orchid Island, off the south-east coast of Taiwan. Lan Yü is the home of the Yami people. They make a meagre living by fishing and planting taro root. The older men still wear loincloths; the women wear shells around their necks and chew betelnut. Next to Lan Yü lies Little Lan Yü, where the spirits of the dead live. Yami children are not allowed to go there.

Michael, a jovial, lanky man, wearing a T-shirt and a baseball cap, handed out copies of *National Geographic* to a group of young men lying down on a wooden platform next to a concrete hut. The platform on stilts, a traditional feature of Yami housing, was built by the men, the concrete hut by the government. Most of the men appeared bored by the magazines, except for one boy of about fourteen, who was fascinated, and asked Michael questions about Vancouver, the Cotswolds, Botswana or whatever happened to catch his eye. He told us in fluent Mandarin that he had failed to get into middle-school. Instead he entered a special government school, where he was taught the necessary skills to work in a fish-processing plant. The plant was still in its planning stage. He had run away from home once, to Taipei, where he was picked up by agents for a sweat-shop. There he was confined virtually as a slave, until he ran away one night, pursued by thugs employed by the boss. 'Taipei was fun,' he said.

When it was time to say goodbye to the boy at the small airport, his parents turned up, both barefoot, the father wearing a loincloth. Michael lined the three of them up for a photograph. They were peering intently into the lens, when there was a sudden commotion in the airport lounge. A Taiwanese tourist was handing out chocolates from a paper bag. He was immediately surrounded by elderly Yami people frantically stretching their hands. The boy's parents joined the fray. The boy looked embarrassed. 'Their thinking is very different from ours,' he said.

He is an extreme example of the Taiwanese conundrum: a man stuck between worlds shaped by others. To try to force him to turn back to the world of his parents, with its spirits and taboos, would be cruel and futile. His thinking is shaped by the official images of the mainland Chinese. He was taught the geography of China at school, not that of Taiwan. He was taught the Three Principles and the heroic struggles of Sun Yat-sen and the Generalissimo. Then there are the images brought by the missionaries. Three North American spinsters live on the island working on a translation into Yami of the New Testament. They must first learn Yami themselves and teach the Yami how to read romanized script. But eventually, they hope to reach 'maybe hundreds of people'. It might not be quite as absurd as it seems. At least it preserves the language and Christianity is perhaps a way for tribes to recover self-esteem. 'The Church,' said Ziro, the social worker, 'helps us think about our identity. It might not solve our problems, but it is better than disappearing without a trace.'

One of the Yami community leaders is a Taiwanese man called Lin Mao-an. A small man in jeans and glasses, he looked like a graduate student or a bookish social worker. Lin's first visit to Lan Yü was on a student excursion. A year or so later, still a student, Lin had a religious vision: 'I thought I could see God, and I cried and cried. Then I asked God about my future, for I was very confused at the time. I cried again and suddenly my future was revealed. I had to do something for the Yami.' He moved to Lan Yü, married a

157

Yami woman and set up a kindergarten. It is a small wooden building in the main village, with children's drawings on the wall, Christian symbols, as well as the obligatory pictures of the Generalissimo and Sun Yat-sen.

Lin does not speak Yami, but believes Yami culture is 'very good'. He established a committee to promote it. The problem is that there is no consensus among the Yami themselves about what Yami culture is. So, says Lin, 'we must define it first.' I asked Lin what he thought about his own past, the culture and traditions of the Taiwanese. He was never much interested in that: 'Perhaps I was anaesthetized by my education, but I don't feel deprived.' Did the Yami feel deprived? No, he said, not much. An attempt was made to get youth groups together to discuss Yami culture, but only four or five people turned up. So why was Lin so interested? He thought for a moment, smiled, and said, 'Well, it is like this. Why do foreigners come to Taiwan to tell us how to be Chinese?' It was a very Taiwanese answer.

TELA ZASLOFF
SAIGON DREAMING

176 rue Pasteur

Our house had once been elegant in the provincial French manner, with balconies and verandas and climbing vines of pink blossoms and servants' quarters in the back. But like all the houses on the street, ours was now surrounded by a high concrete wall with barbed wire across the top.

In the summer of 1964, when we arrived in Saigon, our house belonged to the United States military, whose cheerful Vietnamese employees moved us in. A small, stooping gardener appeared almost every day, his face covered by a straw hat. He never spoke, but tipped his head slightly in our direction and dug assiduously in our small front yard, apparently weeding and caring for the narrow strip of grass. Chi Hai wet-mopped the red tile floors twice a day, or rather it was Chi Ba who mopped them, working under Chi Hai's impatient and sometimes vindictive supervision. The kitchen belonged to Anh Ba, who cooked, shopped, directed meals, and oversaw Chi Hai's service—with continual displeasure.

The stairway to the second floor had two long, polished, cherrywood handrails that were smooth and pleasing to touch. That first evening we tried sitting out on the front balconies, but the blue smoke from misfiring cars and motor scooters drove us indoors. Our bedroom and bath were at the back of the house. We opened the black wooden shutters of our window and looked out at the servants' quarters strung with lines of our clothes, and across to the high wall and roof-top of our unknown neighbour.

Tela Zasloff went with her husband, Joe, to Saigon in 1964, at the age of twenty-five, to conduct a political study of the Vietnamese communists. In February 1965, two months after the Zasloffs had returned to the United States, President Johnson sent the first contingent of American combat forces to Vietnam.

161

Tela Zasloff

Fauna

I do not remember seeing any dogs being walked. Our neighbours were protected by hidden, chained dogs that, judging from the deep barking, must have been German Shepherds. The one Vietnamese neighbour I visited had three small white lap-dogs that suffered from an unsightly mange. Chi Hai and Chi Ba remarked that the disappearance of several small dogs at a house down the street was because they were served up for dinner.

I remember no cats, although the size of the rats caught periodically in our storm drains by the military maintenance crew suggested that a cat population would serve the city well. The trees and flowers were constantly blooming and I would like to imagine that I heard exotic birds outside our windows, but I cannot remember noticing even one. Ponies and bulls with jutting rib-cages hauled firewood and produce to the market-place where mournful trick monkeys could sometimes be seen on the shoulders of their owners, trying to attract children. Once a vendor was selling a long, beautiful striped wildcat in a rhinestone collar; it was obviously ill and doped. When I remarked, '*Il est malade*,' the vendor glowered at me and shook the leash to stir the animal.

Insects were ubiquitous, and attracted to Americans who rejected the old colonial mosquito netting and demanded that all windows be screened. According to an old saying, in your first year in Saigon you ordered another glass when a fly was found in your drink. In the second year, you removed the fly before drinking. In the third year you drank it, fly and all, and found it tasty. Most women occupied themselves at lawn dinner parties by swatting their legs. The best friends to the bitten were the geckos: tan lizards ranging from one or two inches to over a foot in length, which ran over our walls and ceilings and rapidly depleted the bug population with their darting tongues.

In Dalat, a mountain town a short plane-ride from Saigon, the French innkeeper with whom we stayed was puzzled by our shorts, long socks and tennis shoes, and by our request for trail-riding horses. At our insistence, he sent us to a herdsman who laughed at us but took our payment and helped us atop two small grey ponies with sagging backs that jogged reluctantly up and down a few scraggy hills, moving only because their owner ran after them with a switch. A small crowd of country people gathered to watch and giggle. They were complimenting me, the owner reassured us, on my balance when the ride abruptly ended with a cartoon flourish when my husband's groaning pony sat down like a camel and refused to move. (On that same day, in Saigon, Generals Lam Van Phat and Duong Van Duc led a coup against the Khanh government. The next day, under American pressure and the threat of bombardment by Air Vice Marshall Nguyen Cao Ky, the generals backed down.)

Beggars

I was not prepared for the beggars or my reaction to them. They were mostly children, crippled, maimed or diseased. Others relied on a practised beseeching voice. All were horribly aggressive. It was impossible, for an American who had recently arrived, to walk along certain sidewalks.

There was one legless nine-year-old boy who pushed himself on a skateboard with great speed between the Hotel Continental, where he operated among the tables on the veranda, and the Caravelle, where he rolled among newsmen arranging airline tickets in the ground-floor travel office. I avoided him regularly. One afternoon I went to the central market with Chi Hai. I never found the market a pleasant experience; it was invariably hot and crowded, full of rotting fish and vegetables, and one had to haggle continually. A ragged girl of about ten pulled on my arm and held out her hand which had a few piastres in it given by others. I took one and thanked her and pretended to put it in my pocket. She looked confused. I felt I had made my point. On the same street a healthy-looking boy followed me for two blocks asking for money in a low whine. I ripped the cellophane wrapper off a pack of gum and put the crinkly piece of paper in his outstretched hand. For a few seconds he stared at it, then looked me brightly in the eye and laughed. He turned the paper over and over in mock wonder and pressed it to his face with noises of contrived gratitude. I laughed with him.

How do I explain my behaviour? I remember a need to escape the degradation in which I was being invited to participate. Perhaps that is why I wanted to laugh ironically with these children. The boy with the cellophane seems to have shared my feeling for the short time that he performed his fake gratitude act. I recognized the same defusing irony twenty-four years later when in New York City. I felt my purse lighten and turned around, catching a man lifting my wallet out by the corner, and I smiled and held out my hand. He politely returned the wallet and said, 'Oh, excuse me.' 'That's quite all right,' I answered, and we quietly parted, like slight acquaintances who had exchanged remarks on the weather.

In Saigon I was angry at the con game substituted for real misery and furious at the feeling I was being held personally accountable. But another voice murmured to me every day I walked those streets that I had played a part in producing these sorry human beings.

In Concert

Soon after we moved into our house, I rented a piano. It must have been the overheated atmosphere of our Saigon existence that created this sudden thirst for playing classical music. Every day I played for hours during the cool time—relentless Bach preludes and fugues, Chopin études, a Mozart concerto that always became most exciting at the wrenching modulations.

Before renting a piano, I borrowed one. The day after Congress had passed the Gulf of Tonkin resolution and the United States began bombing North Vietnam's bases, I met a young Vietnamese woman who lived nearby in a large apartment building owned by her family. She was trained at a Paris conservatory and agreed to let me play on her twin black concert grands, Yamahas, sitting back to back in a large airy room. There was a picture of Mary Baker Eddy on the wall. The tile floor opened on to a balcony above a courtyard that was always crowded with laundry and maids and boisterous children and cages of small song-birds.

My hostess was always dressed like a cinema version of a Sorbonne student, in a grey turtle-neck sweater and dark pants, her long hair, worn in no particular style, falling across a sombre face. She spoke in short bursts of English or French, and we were never able to conduct a continuous conversation. One day she mentioned that she played a Tchaikovsky piano concerto for eight hours straight as the background for a film. On another occasion she pointed to the Eddy picture on the wall and stated simply, apropos of nothing, that she was a Christian Scientist.

The second day I went to her apartment she asked me to join her in a benefit recital sponsored by the Grey Ladies, a voluntary group of Saigon wives of senior Vietnamese military officers whose purpose was to do good works for the victims of the war. My hostess needed piano accompaniment for her performance of the Mozart Piano Concerto in A Major and also a soloist to share the programme with her: I was invited to play two or three pieces. I chose Chopin's *Chromatic Etude*, a Bach prelude and fugue, and a humorous Roy Harris suite. My partner would supplement the Mozart concerto with Debussy, Liszt and Fauré.

I practised with enthusiasm over the next three months—at my partner's house or later, at a small conservatory near the Saigon Cathedral. I was relaxed, assuming that the audience would be uncritical. My partner appeared less frequently and often cancelled our practice sessions, whether out of tension or apathy I never knew.

Critics of varying severity listened to us occasionally. My partner's husband, who was in the South Vietnamese navy, commented vaguely in his genteel manner. Her father, who had just declined an invitation to be a minister in the short-lived Phan Khac Suu government, bowed and smiled politely. A half-blind Czech listened to us and advised sourly that we practise at least twenty more times. He would be reviewing the concert for the local French-language newspaper. Two days before the recital, a small man in a French suit and shiny shoes, said that our rendition of the Mozart was '*pas mal*' but that it could be played only by men.

The recital was cancelled several times, apparently due to the street demonstrations or, more to the point, to the chairwoman's concern that she would not be able to sell enough tickets.

For all the uncertainty in the planning stages, the event passed smoothly. About 300 people attended—Vietnamese, Americans and French, including many children. They applauded loudly, and some said they were touched to see such a Vietnamese-American partnership. Mrs Westmoreland, wife of the commander of the US forces in Vietnam, sat in the front row. My riding instructor, a captain in the US Army, sat silently in the back, and Chi Hai walked in late with her children, dressed in flowered silks and straw hats.

For an hour and a half the music carried us all out of Saigon. It was the longest time during our stay in which I was able to forget the differences between myself and the people around me.

Demonstrations

The odd aspect of letters from home was their view that we were living in constant danger. Certainly in 1964 there were demonstrations against the Khanh government, and people were killed in street riots. Students walked together in sullen groups, carrying clubs and bricks, and police, in routing protesting Buddhist monks and nuns, were known to injure and sometimes kill. But we saw no terrorism and the closest we got to violence was the Sunday morning before Thanksgiving when we got caught in a tear-gas cloud rolling down our street, the cannisters having just been thrown by soldiers in full battle gear, holding at bay a small group of sign-carriers come to watch the swearing in of the new civilian government. The gas stung our eyes and throats and forced us inside. Afterwards, at a dinner, an American CIA agent claimed that the Viet Cong were behind the demonstrations.

The largest one we observed was one morning in August. We heard chanting and ran out of the gate to see thousands of students marching down rue Pasteur, led by professors and student policemen in orange-and-yellow arm bands. They were commemorating the death of a Vietnamese girl who had immolated herself the year before. But it was more than an anniversary; the demonstrators were demanding democracy, a free press, open religion, a representative legislature—the elimination of the military dictatorship. A crowd of 25,000 reached the Presidential Palace. President Khanh made the mistake of coming out to face the student leaders. He looked small and unimpressive with his sparse goatee and his sloping shoulders. He climbed on a green car to speak. One student waved a copy of the Vung Tao Charter which Khanh had just promulgated to establish his authority (the students later put a match to it). Khanh was incoherent, shouting slogans about freedom and fighting the enemy. The bodyguards, weaponless and bewildered, and the arm-banded student police, pushed at the crowd and after ten minutes, Khanh disappeared back into the Palace.

Newsmen climbed into the trees for a better view. We stood beside a grey-hooded Buddhist nun and novitiate child. A young girl with bad teeth felt inexpertly along the side of my skirt for a pocket to pick. I caught her hand and shook my head, partly because the skirt had no pockets. And then a sudden downpour broke up the crowd. The hard rain soaked us all and it was useless seeking cover. That afternoon the news was that Khanh had stepped down, and that the military council would elect a chief of state and arrange elections for a national assembly. Khanh in fact was to control the Saigon government for six more months. He was then forced to flee the country following the coup plotted by Colonel Thao. (In a 1983 report, Khanh was managing a small restaurant in West Palm Beach, living among old photographs and souvenirs.)

We walked home that night through deserted streets, fatigued from the tension. The day before a bomb in the Eden Theatre had killed a man passing by on a motorcycle. The day after, a 'plastique' planted on the fifth floor of the Hotel Caravelle wounded five guests. Three days later, during street battles among students and hoodlums with clubs and knives, a fourteen-year-old boy slipped while running away and was hacked to pieces.

Tela Zasloff

Xenophobia

Hué was the ancient imperial capital of Vietnam, where the Gia Long dynasty began in 1802 and ended in 1954. To rebuff Europeans in Asia, Emperor Gia Long and his successor Minh Mang followed a policy of isolationism. Hué was built as a walled city, like Beijing, and its rule was Confucian, highly structured and static, intolerant of innovation or the West.

Hué was in the centre of Vietnam near the Seventeenth Parallel. Ho Chi Minh was born just outside it, where his father was an official in the imperial court and where Ho attended a French school at a time of dissidence and political turmoil.

Hué was the site of two of the most bitter conflagrations of the Vietnam War. During the Tet offensive of January 1968, when the communists besieged all United States and South Vietnamese strongholds simultaneously, the battle for Hué became the worst bloodbath of the war, with unprecedented atrocities committed during the twenty-five days the communists held the city.

Earlier, in May 1963, the Buddhists' call for national unity was made in Hué, where several thousand gathered to celebrate the Buddha's birthday. The Catholic mayor ordered five armoured cars to disperse the crowd, and a woman and eight children were killed. The protests of the next few weeks were followed by more brutal repression by the Ngo Dinh Diem regime. In June 1963, the first Buddhist monk immolated himself on a Saigon street in protest against the Diem government.

A year later, we went to Hué for two days, invited by a poetic German doctor teaching at the medical school who wanted to show us the beauty of Hué's temples and palaces. We were then taken to a deserted sports club veranda for lunch and then to our host's small house to nap under mosquito netting in the intense heat of early afternoon. At about three o'clock we set out for a walk.

We ambled along a dirt road beside a narrow, muddy river. A few people and vehicles moved about slowly. After about fifteen minutes we began to draw a small crowd of children.

They were silent at first. Some wore old cotton shirts and trousers, and others, perched on their older sisters' hips, nothing at all. They kept our pace, first behind and then beside us, and watched us with grim, old-people's eyes even though some of them were grinning. The pack grew and began hooting 'Mee-Hello-OK'. I had become the object of their attention. Someone was kicking rocks at my feet. A few became bolder and knocked into me, touching my bare upper arms. Others started throwing pebbles at my back and legs. Around the edges of the crowd, their parents had joined, with sombre faces and folded arms, watching intently but not calling off the children.

A rage rose in my throat. I shouted at the nearest and pushed to the ground a girl of about five who had grabbed on to the back of my skirt. This brought more hooting. A vision arose in my mind of driving the whole crowd into the muddy river with fire-hoses. My companions advised that I should act unconcerned, and our host tried ordering them away in Vietnamese. We finally flagged down a *cyclo-pousse* and returned home.

I remember nothing else of the visit. Years later there was a report that after the Tet offensive the bodies of a German doctor, his wife and two German colleagues teaching at the medical school in Hué were found in a shallow pit.

There had been occasions in Saigon when we had also provoked laughter and finger-pointing. There was the afternoon we had tried to ride double on a flimsy Saigon bicycle and the poor vehicle bent in two. This had produced loud giggles, and it was indeed funny. Americans were also laughed at if caught in heavy rain. Once I took a taxi to the Chinese section to investigate a piano factory and hurried away finding it too primitive for my needs. A group of children on the sidewalk knocked on the taxi windows and opened the door as the car pulled away. They shouted a sing-song taunt before the old man building the pianos ordered them back into the shop.

Even so, Saigon still had a befuddled graciousness, something like that of the ageing ladies of Tennessee Williams who, inventing their own salvation, court outsiders, trying to maintain a romance about their pasts. In Saigon the courtship was born out of mutual need; the natural hostility of the Vietnamese to a foreign presence was muted, ubiquitous but disguised, made ambiguous by the history of the city that emanated from the sidewalks of rue Catinat and the elegant French-built buildings and schools as well as the bright new army and roads contributed by the Americans. For a very long time Saigon had spoken Vietnamese with a foreign accent.

The older Vietnam had risen in Hué and struck us across the face.

On our last day in Saigon, our staff and friends accompanied us to the airport. Our photographs show that everyone was smiling. But I remember that their eyes looked sombre and anxious: the future seemed grey and unstable. I recall shaking the hands of Chi Hai and Chi Ba, thinking of the Saigon-made tweed suits and Thai silk dress in our suitcases, the paintings and cloth and Cambodian rubbings being shipped home. Half an hour after the party left, we waited for a delayed plane. I glanced idly at the strangers around us: peasants with bundled straw baskets and food boxes and sleeping babies; soldiers smoking and pacing; fashionably dressed families dealing with travel agents with restrained impatience. As I looked around, I was suddenly struck by a powerful revulsion for every person in the place, a blind prejudice against the whole people, the whole country.

Those around were unaware and unconcerned. The official in military uniform, who handed back our papers with a curt nod, unlocked the high chain-link fence that was the departure gate, hurried us through and shut it behind us with a clang.

In Britain it had been a year without summer. Wet spring had merged imperceptibly into bleak autumn. For months the sky had remained a depthless grey. Sometimes it rained, but mostly it was just dull, a land without shadows. It was like living inside Tupperware. And here suddenly the sun was dazzling in its intensity. Iowa was hysterical with colour and light. Roadside barns were a glossy red, the sky a deep, hypnotic blue; fields of mustard and green stretched out before me. Flecks of mica glittered in the rolling road. And here and there in the distance mighty grain elevators, the cathedrals of the Middle West, the ships of the prairie seas, drew the sun's light and bounced it back as pure white. Squinting in the unaccustomed brilliance, I followed the highway to Otley.

My intention was to retrace the route my father always took to my grandparents' house in Winfield—through Prairie City, Pella, Oskaloosa, Hedrick, Brighton, Coppock, Wayland and Olds. The sequence was tattooed on my memory. Always having been a passenger before, I had never paid much attention to the road, so I was surprised to find that I kept coming up against odd turns and abrupt T-junctions, requiring me to go left here for a couple of miles, then right for a few miles, then left again and so on. It would have been much more straightforward to take Highway 92 to Ainsworth and then head south to Mount Pleasant. I couldn't imagine by what method of reasoning my father had ever settled on this route, and now of course I never would know. This seemed a pity, particularly as there was almost nothing he would have liked better than to cover the dining-room table with maps and consider at length possible routings. In this he was like most Midwesterners. Directions are very important to them. They have an innate need to be oriented, even in their anecdotes. Any story related by a Midwesterner will wander off at some point into a thicket of interior monologue along the lines of 'We were staying at a hotel that was eight blocks north-east of the state capitol building. Come to think of it, it was north-west. And I think it was probably more like nine blocks. And this woman without any clothes on, naked as the day she was born except for a coonskin cap, came running at us from the south-west . . . or was it the south-east?' If there are two Midwesterners present and they both witnessed the incident, you can just about write off the anecdote because they will spend the rest of the afternoon arguing points of the compass and will never get back to the original story. You can always tell a Midwestern couple in Europe because they will be standing on a traffic island in the middle of a busy intersection looking at a wind-blown map and arguing over which way is west. European cities, with their wandering streets and undisciplined alleys, drive Midwesterners practically insane.

This geographical obsession probably has something to do with the absence of landmarks throughout middle America. I had forgotten just how flat and empty it is. Stand on two phone books almost anywhere in Iowa and you get a view. From where I was now I could look out on a sweep of landscape about the size of Belgium, but there was nothing on it except for a few widely separated farms, some scattered stands of trees and two water-towers, brilliant silver glints signifying distant, unseen towns. Far off in the middle distance a cloud of dust chased a car up a gravel road. The only things that stood out from the landscape were the grain elevators, but even they looked all the same, and there was nothing much to distinguish one view from another.

And it's so quiet. Apart from the ceaseless fidgeting of the corn, there is not a sound. Somebody could sneeze in a house three miles away and you would hear it ('Bless you!' 'Thank you!'). It must nearly drive you crazy to live a life so devoid of stimulus, where no passing aeroplane ever draws your gaze and no car horns honk, where time shuffles forward so slowly that you half expect to find the people still watching *Ozzie and Harriet* on TV and voting for Eisenhower. ('I don't know how far you folks in Des Moines have got, but we're only up to 1958 here in Fudd County.')

Small towns are equally unhelpful in offering distinguishing features. About all that separates them are their names. They always have a gas station, a grocery store, a grain elevator, a place selling farm equipment and fertilizers, and something improbable like a microwave-oven dealer or a dry-cleaner's, so you can say to yourself as you glide through town: 'Now what would they be doing with a dry-cleaner's in Fungus City?'

Every fourth or fifth community will be a county town, built around a square. A handsome brick court-house with a Civil War cannon and a monument to the dead of at least two wars will stand on one side of the square and on the other sides will be a five and dime, a luncheonette, two banks, a hardware store, a Christian bookstore, a barber's, a couple of hairdressers and a place selling the sort of men's clothing that only someone from a very small town would wear. At least two of the businesses will be called Vern's. The central area of the square will be a park, with fat trees and a bandstand and a pole with an American flag and scattered benches full of old men in John Deere caps sitting around talking about the days when they had something else to do other than sit around and talk about the days when they had something else to do. Time in these places creaks along.

The best county town in Iowa is Pella, forty miles south-east of Des Moines. Pella was founded by Dutch immigrants and every May it holds a big tulip festival for which they get somebody important like the major of The Hague to fly in and praise their bulbs. I used to like Pella when I was little because many of the residents put little windmills in their front-yards, which made it kind of interesting. I wouldn't say it made it *outstandingly* interesting, but you learned from an early age to take what pleasures you could find on any trip across Iowa. Besides, Pella had a Dairy Queen on the edge of town where my father would sometimes stop and buy us ice-cream cones dipped in chocolate, and for this alone I have always felt a special fondness for the place. So I was pleased to note, as I rolled into the town on this fine September morning, that there were still windmills whirling in many a front-yard. I stopped at the square and got out to stretch my legs. Being a Sunday, the old men from the square had the day off— they would be on sleeping-in-front-of-the-TV duty all day—but in every other respect Pella was as perfect as I remembered it. The square was thick with trees and flower-beds of blazing salvias and glowing marigolds. It had its own windmill, a handsome green one with white blades, nearly full-sized, standing in one corner. The stores around the square were of the cereal-box architecture favoured by small-town stores throughout the Midwest, but with gingerbread cornices and other cheery embellishments. Every business had a solid, trustworthy Dutch name: Pardekooper's Drug Store, Jaarsma Bakery, Van Gorp Insurers, Gosselink's Christian Book Store, Vander Ploeg Bakery. All were shut, of course. Sundays are still closely observed in places like Pella. Indeed, the whole town was eerily quiet. It was steeped in that kind of dead silence that makes you begin to wonder, if you are of a suitably hysterical nature, if perhaps everybody has been poisoned in the night by a leak of odourless gas—which even now could be taking insidious control of your own central nervous system—turning Pella into a kind of Pompeii of the plains. I briefly imagined people from all over coming to look at the victims and being especially enthralled at the worried-looking young man in spectacles on the town square, clutching his throat and trying to get his car door open. But then I saw a man walking a dog at the far end of the square and realized that any danger was safely past.

I hadn't intended to linger, but it was such a splendid morning that I wandered off down a nearby street, past neat wooden-framed houses with cupolas and gables and front porches with two-seater swings that creaked in the breeze. There was no other sound, apart from the scuffling of my feet through dried leaves. At the bottom of the street, I came across Central College, a small institution run by the Dutch Reformed Church, with a campus of redbrick buildings overlooking a serpentine stream with an arching wooden foot-bridge. The whole place was as tranquil as a double dose of Valium. It looked like the sort of tidy, friendly, clean-thinking college that Clark Kent would have attended. I crossed the bridge and at the far side of the campus found further evidence that I was not the only living person in Pella. From an open window high up in a dormitory building came the sound of a stereo turned up far too loud. It blared for a moment—something by Frankie Goes to Hollywood, I believe—and then from someplace indiscernible there came a booming voice that said: 'IF YOU DON'T TURN THAT THING THE FUCK OFF RIGHT NOW I'M GONNA COME OVER THERE AND POUND YOUR HEAD IN!' It was the voice of a large person—someone, I fancied, with the nickname Moose. Immediately the music stopped and Pella slept again.

I continued on east, through Oskaloosa, Fremont, Hedrick, Martinsburg. The names were familiar, but the towns themselves awoke few memories. By this stage on most trips as a child I was on the floor in a boredom-induced stupor, calling out at fifteen-second intervals: 'How much longer? When are we going to be there? I'm bored. I feel sick. How much longer? When are we going to be there?' I vaguely recognized a bend in the road near Coppock, where we once spent four hours caught in a blizzard waiting for a snow-plough to come through, and several spots where we had paused to let my sister throw up, including a gas station at Martinsburg where she tumbled out of the car and was lavishly sick in the direction of a pump attendant's ankles (boy did that guy dance!), and another at Wayland where my father nearly left me at the side of the road after discovering that I had passed the time by working loose all the rivets on one of the back-door panels, exposing an interesting view of the interior mechanisms, but unfortunately rendering both the window and door forever inoperable.

It wasn't until I reached the turning off for Winfield, just past Olds, a place where my father would announce with a sort of delirious joy that we were practically there, that I felt a pang of recognition. I had not been down this road for at least a dozen years, but its gentle slopes and isolated farms were as familiar to me as my own left leg. My heart soared. This was like going back in time. I was about to be a boy again.

Arriving in Winfield was always thrilling. Dad would turn off Highway 78 and bounce us down a rough gravel road at far too high a speed, throwing up clouds of white dust, and then to my mother's unfailing alarm would drive with evident insanity towards some railroad tracks on a blind bend in the road, remarking gravely: 'I hope there's not a train coming.' My mother didn't discover until years later that there were only two trains a day along those tracks, both in the dead of night. Beyond the tracks, standing alone in a neglected field, was a Victorian mansion like the one in the Charles Addams cartoons in the *New Yorker*. No one had lived in it for decades, but it was still full of furniture, under dank sheets. My sister and brother and I used to climb in through a broken window and look through trunks of musty clothes and old *Collier's* magazines and photographs of strangely worried-looking people. Upstairs was a bedroom in which, according to my brother, lay the shrivelled body of the last occupant, a woman who had died of heart-break after being abandoned at the altar. We never went in there, though once, when I was about four, my brother peered through the keyhole, let out a howl, cried 'She's coming!' and ran headlong down the stairs. Whimpering, I followed, squirting urine at every step.

Beyond the mansion was a wide field, full of black-and-white cows, and beyond that was my grandparents' house, pretty and white beneath a canopy of trees, with a big red barn and acres of lawn. My grandparents were always waiting at the gate. I don't know whether they could see us coming and raced to their positions or whether they just waited there hour after hour. Quite possibly the latter because, let's face it, they didn't have a whole lot else to do. And then it would be four or five days of fun. My grandfather had a Model T Ford, which he let us kids drive around the yard, to the distress of his chickens and the older women. In the winter he would attach a sleigh to the back and take us for long, cold rides down snowy roads. In the evenings we would all play cards around the kitchen table and stay up late. It was always Christmas at my grandparents' house, or Thanksgiving, or the Fourth of July, or somebody's birthday. There was always happiness there.

When we arrived, my grandmother would scuttle off to pull something freshly baked out of the oven. This was always something unusual. My grandmother was the only person I ever knew—possibly the only person who ever lived—who actually made things from the recipes on the backs of food packets. These dishes always had names like 'Rice Krispies 'n' Banana Chunks Upside Down Cake' or 'Del Monte Lima Bean 'n' Pretzels Party Snacks'. Generally they consisted of suspiciously large amounts of the manufacturer's own products, usually in combinations you wouldn't think of except perhaps in an especially severe famine. The one thing to be said for these dishes was that they were novel. When my grandmother offered you a steaming slab of cake or wedge of pie it might contain almost anything—Niblets sweet corn, chocolate chips, Spam, diced carrots, peanut butter. Generally it would have some Rice Krispies in it somewhere. My grandmother was particularly partial to Rice Krispies and would add a couple of shovelfuls to whatever she made, even if the recipe didn't call for it. She was about as bad a cook as you can be without actually being hazardous.

It all seems so long ago now. And it was. It was so long ago, in fact, that my grandparents had a crank telephone, the kind that hung on the wall and had a handle you turned and said: 'Mabel, get me Gladys Scribbage. I want to ask her how she makes her "Frosted Flakes 'n' Cheez-Whizz Party Nuggets".' And it would turn out that Gladys Scribbage was already listening in, or somebody else listening in would know how to make 'Frosted Flakes 'n' Cheez-Whizz Party Nuggets.' Everybody listened in. My grandmother often listened in when things were slow around the house, covering the mouthpiece with a hand and relaying to the rest of the room vivid accounts of colonic irrigations, prolapsed wombs, husbands who ran off to Burlington with the barmaid from Vern's Uptown Tavern and Supper Club, and other crises of small-town life. We always had to maintain the strictest silence during these sessions. I could never entirely understand why because if things got really juicy my grandmother would often butt in. 'Well, I think Merle's a real skunk,' she would say. 'Yes, that's right, it's Maude Bryson here, and I just want to say that I think he's an absolute stinker to do that to poor Pearl. And I'll tell you something else, Mabel, you know you could get those support bras a dollar cheaper in Columbus Junction.' In about 1962 the telephone company came and put a normal phone without a party-line in my grandmother's house, possibly at the request of the rest of the town. It drove a hole right through her life from which she never entirely recovered.

I didn't really expect my grandparents to be waiting for me at the gate, on account of them both having been dead for many years. But I suppose I had vaguely hoped that another nice old couple might be living there now and would invite me in to look around and share my reminiscences. Perhaps they would let me be their grandson. At the very least, I had assumed that my grandparents' house would be just as I had last seen it.

It was not to be. The road leading to the house was still gravelled with gleaming gypsum pebbles and still threw up satisfying clouds of dust, but the railroad tracks were gone. There was no sign that they had ever been there. The Victorian mansion was gone too, replaced by a ranch-house-style home with cars and propane-gas cylinders scattered around the yard like a toddler's playthings. Worse still, the field of cows was now an estate of box-houses. My grandparents' home had stood well outside the town, a cool island of trees in an ocean of fields. Now cheap little houses crowded in on it from all sides. With shock, I realized that the barn was gone. Some jerk had torn down my barn! And the house itself—well, it was a shack. Paint had abandoned it in chunks. Bushes had been pointlessly uprooted, trees had been chopped down. The grass was high and littered with overspill from the house. I stopped the car on the road and gaped. I cannot describe the sense of loss. Half my memories were inside that house. After a moment a hugely overweight woman in pink shorts, talking on a phone with an apparently endless cord, came and stood in the open doorway and stared at me, wondering what I was doing staring at her.

I drove on into the town. When I was growing up Main Street in Winfield had two grocery stores, a variety store, a tavern, a pool hall, a newspaper, a bank, a barbershop, a post office, two gas stations—all the things you would expect of any thriving little town. Everyone shopped locally; everyone knew everyone else. Now all that was left was a tavern and a place selling farm equipment. There were half a dozen vacant lots, full of patchy grass, where buildings had been torn down and never replaced. Most of the remaining buildings were dark and boarded up. It was like an abandoned film set which had long since been left to decay.

I couldn't understand what had happened. People now must have to drive thirty miles to buy a loaf of bread. Outside the tavern a group of young thuggy-looking motorcyclists were hanging out. I was going to stop to ask them what had happened to their town, but one of them, seeing me slow down, gave me the finger. For no reason. He was about fourteen. Abruptly, I drove on, back out towards Highway 78, past the scattered farms and gentle slopes that I knew like my own left leg. It was the first time in my life that I had turned my back on a place knowing that I would never see it again. It was all very sad, but I should have known better. As I always used to tell Thomas Wolfe, there are three things you just can't do in life. You can't beat the phone company, you can't make a waiter see you until he's ready to see you, and you can't go home again.

I drove on, without the radio or much in the way of thoughts, to Mount Pleasant, where I stopped for coffee. I had the Sunday *New York Times* with me—one of the greatest improvements in life since I had been away was that you could now buy the *New York Times* out of machines on the day of publication in a place like Iowa, an extraordinary feat of distribution—and I spread out with it in a booth. Boy, do I love the Sunday *New York Times*. Apart from its many virtues as a newspaper, there is just something wonderfully reassuring about its very bulk. The issue in front of me must have weighed ten or twelve pounds. It could've stopped a bullet at twenty yards. I read once that it takes 75,000 trees to produce one issue of the Sunday *New York Times*—and it's well worth every trembling leaf. So what if our grandchildren have no oxygen to breathe? Fuck 'em.

My favourite parts of the *Times* are the peripheral bits—the parts that are so dull and obscure that they exert a kind of hypnotic fascination, like the home improvements column ('All You Need to Know About Fixings and Fastenings') and the stamps column ('Post Office Marks Twenty-Five Years of Aeronautic Issues'). Above all, I love the advertising supplements. If a Bulgarian asked me what life was like in America, I would without hesitation tell him to get hold of a stack of *New York Times* advertising supplements. They show a life of richness and variety beyond the wildest dreams of most foreigners. As if to illustrate my point, the issue before me contained a gift catalogue from the Zwingle Company of New York offering scores of products of the things-you-never-knew-you-needed variety—musical shoe-trees, an umbrella with a transistor radio in the handle, an electric nail-buffer. What a great country! My favourite was a small electric hot-plate you could put on your desk to keep your coffee from going cold. This must be a real boon to people with brain damage, the sort of injuries that lead them to wander off and neglect their beverages. And epileptics all over America must be feeling equally grateful. ('Dear Zwingle Company: I can't tell you how many times I have come around from a *grand mal* seizure to find myself lying on the floor thinking: "Oh, God, I bet my coffee's gone cold again."') Really, who buys these things—silver toothpicks and monogrammed underpants and mirrors that say 'Man of the Year' on them? I have often thought that if I ran one of these companies I would produce a polished mahogany plaque with a brass plate on it saying: 'Hey, how about me? I paid $22.95 for this completely useless piece of crap.' I'm certain they would sell like hot cakes.

Once, in a deranged moment, I bought something myself from one of these catalogues knowing deep in my mind that it would end in heart-break. It was a little reading light that you clipped on to your book so as not to disturb your bedmate as she slumbered beside you. In this respect it was outstanding because it barely worked. The light it cast was absurdly feeble (in the catalogue it looked like the sort of thing you could signal ships with if you got lost at sea) and left all but the first two lines of a page in darkness. I have seen more luminous insects. After about four minutes its little beam fluttered and failed altogether, and it has never been used again. And the thing is that I knew all along that this was how it was going to end, that it would all be a bitter disappointment. On second thoughts, if I ever ran one of those companies I would just send people an empty box with a note in it saying: 'We have decided not to send you the item you've ordered because, as you well know, it would never properly work and you would only be disappointed. So let this be a lesson to you for the future.'

From the Zwingle catalogue I moved on to the food and household products advertisements. There is usually a wodge of these bright and glossy inducements to try out exciting new products—things with names like Hunk o' Meat Beef Stew 'n' Gravy ('with rich 'n' meaty chunks of beef-textured fibre') and Sniffa-Snax ('An Exciting New Snack Treat You Take Through the Nose!') and Country Sunshine Honey-Toasted Wheat Nut 'n' Sugar Bits Breakfast Cereal ('Now with Vitamin-Enriched Chocolate Covered Raisin Substitute!'). I am endlessly fascinated by these new products. Clearly some time ago makers and consumers of American junk food passed jointly through some kind of sensibility barrier in the endless quest for new taste sensations. Now they are a little like those desperate junkies who have tried every known drug and are finally reduced to mainlining bathroom bowl cleanser in an effort to get still higher. All over America you can see countless flabby-butted couples quietly searching supermarket shelves for new combinations of flavours, hoping to find some

183

untried product that will tingle in their mouths and excite, however briefly, their leaden taste-buds.

The competition for this market is intense. The food inserts not only offered fifty-cent discounts and the like, but also if you sent off two or three labels the manufacturers would despatch to you a Hunk o' Meat Beach Towel, or Country Sunshine Matching Apron and Oven Mitt, or a Sniffa-Snax hot-plate for keeping your coffee warm while you slipped in and out of consciousness from a surfeit of blood sugar. Interestingly, the advertisements for dog food were much the same, except that they weren't usually chocolate-flavoured. In fact, every single product—from the lemon-scented toilet-bowl cleansers to the scent-o-pine trash-bags—promised to give you a brief buzz. It's no wonder that so many Americans have a glazed look. They are completely junked out.

I drove on south on Highway 218 to Keokuk. This stretch of the road was marked on my map as a scenic route, though these things are decidedly relative. Talking about a scenic route in south-east Iowa is like talking about a good Barry Manilow album. You have to make certain allowances. Compared with an afternoon in a darkened room, it wasn't bad. But compared with, say, the coast road along the Sorrentine peninsula, it was perhaps a little tame. Certainly it didn't strike me as being any more or less scenic than any of the other roads I had been on today. Keokuk is a Mississippi River town where Iowa, Illinois and Missouri face each other across a broad bend in the river. I was heading towards Hannibal in Missouri and was hoping to see a bit of the town en route to the bridge south. But before I knew it, I found myself on a bridge going east to Illinois. I was so disconcerted by this that I only caught a glimpse of the river, a glistening smear of brown stretching off in two directions, and then, chagrined, I was in Illinois. I had really looked forward to seeing the Mississippi. Crossing it as a child had always been an adventure. Dad would call: 'Here's the Mississippi, kids!' and we would scramble to the window to find ourselves on a bridge practically in the clouds, so high it made our breath catch, and the silvery river far, far below, wide, majestic, serene, going about its timeless business of just rolling along. You could see for miles—a novel experience in Iowa. You could see barges and islands and riverside towns. It looked wonderful. And then, abruptly, you were in Illinois and it was flat and full of corn and you realized with a sinking heart that that was it. That was your visual stimulation for the day. Now you had hundreds more miles of arid cornland to cross before you would experience even the most fractional sense of pleasure.

And now here I was in Illinois, and it was flat and full of corn and boring. A childlike voice in my head cried: 'When are we going to be there? I'm bored. Let's go home. When are we going to be there?' Having confidently expected at this stage to be in Missouri, I had my book of maps opened to the Missouri page, so I pulled over to the side of the road, in a state of some petulance, to make a cartographical adjustment. A sign just ahead of me said: 'Buckle Up. Its the Law in Illinois.' Clearly, however, it was not an offence to be unable to punctuate. Frowning, I studied my maps. If I turned off at Hamilton, just down the road, I could drive along the east bank of the river and cross into Missouri at Quincy. It was even marked on the map as a scenic route, perhaps my blundering would turn out to be no bad thing.

I followed the road through Warsaw, a rundown little river town. A steep hill plunged down towards the river, but then turned inland and again I caught no more than a glimpse of the river. Almost immediately, the landscape spread out into a broad alluvial plain. The sun was sinking in the sky. To the left hills rose up, flecked with trees that were just beginning to show a blush of autumn colour. To the right the land was as flat as a table-top. Teams of combine harvesters laboured in the fields, kicking up dust, working late to bring in the harvest. In the far distance, grain elevators caught the fading sun and glowed an opalescent white, as if lit from within. Somewhere out there, unseen, was the river.

I drove on. The road was completely unsignposted. They do this to you a lot in America, particularly on country roads that go from nowhere to nowhere. You are left to rely on your own sense of direction to find your way—which in my case, let us not forget, had only recently delivered me to the wrong state. I calculated that if I were going south the sun should be to my right (a conclusion I reached by imagining myself in a tiny car driving across a big map of America), but the road twisted and wandered, causing the sun to drift teasingly in front of me, first to this side of the road, then to that. For the first time all day, I had a sense of being in the heart of a vast continent, in the middle of nowhere.

Abruptly the highway turned to gravel. Gypsum nuggets, jagged as arrowheads, flew up against the underside of the car and made a fearful din. I had visions of hose-pipes rupturing, hot oil spraying everywhere, me rolling to a steamy, hissing halt out here on this desolate road. The wandering sun was just settling on to the horizon, splashing the sky with faint pinks. Uneasily I drove on, and steeled myself for the prospect of a night spent beneath the stars, with dog-like animals sniffing at my feet and snakes finding warmth up a trouser leg. Ahead of me on the road an advancing storm of dust became after a moment a pick-up truck, which passed in a hell-bent fashion, spraying the car with rocky projectiles, which thumped against the sides and bounced off the windows with a cracking sound, and then left me adrift in a cloud of dust. I trundled on, peering helplessly through the murk. It cleared just in time to show me that I was twenty feet from a T-junction with a stop sign. I was going fifty miles an hour, which on gravel leaves you with a stopping distance of about three miles. I jumped on the brakes with all my feet and made a noise like Tarzan missing a vine as the car went into a skid. It slid sideways past the stop sign and out on to a paved highway, where it came to a halt, rocking gently from side to side. At that instant an enormous semi-trailer truck—all silver horns and flashing lights—blared mightily at me as it swept past, setting the car to rocking again. Had I slid out on to the highway three seconds earlier it would have crushed the car into something about the size of a stock cube. I pulled on to the shoulder and got out to examine the damage. It looked as if the car had been dive-bombed with bags of flour. Bits of raw metal showed through where paint had been pinged away. I thanked God that my mother was so much smaller than me. I sighed, suddenly feeling lost and far from home, and noticed ahead a road sign pointing the way to Quincy. I had come to a halt facing in the right direction, so at least something had come of it.

It was time to stop. Just down the road stood a little town, which I shall call Dullard lest the people recognize themselves and take me to court or come to my house and batter me with baseball bats. On the edge of town was an old motel which looked pretty seedy, though judging by the absence of charred furniture in the front yard it was clearly a step up from the sort of place my dad would have chosen. I pulled on to the gravel drive and went inside. A woman of about seventy-five was sitting behind the desk. She wore butterfly eyeglasses and had a beehive hair-do. She was doing one of those books that require you to find words in a mass of letters and circle them. I think it was called *Word Puzzles for Morons*.

'Help yew?' she drawled without looking up.

'I'd like a room for the night, please.'

'That'll be thirty-eight dollars and fifty cents,' she replied, as her pen fell greedily on the word YUP.

I was nonplussed. In my day a motel room cost about twelve dollars, but I was miles from anywhere. 'Yes, please,' I said contritely. I signed in and crunched across the gravel to my *suite de nuit*. There appeared to be no other customers. I went into my room with my bag and had a look around, as you do in a new place. There was a black-and-white TV, which appeared to get only one channel, and three bent coat-hangers. The bathroom mirror was cracked, and the shower curtains didn't match.

I had a shower and went to check out the town. I had a meal of gristle and baked wiffle-ball at a place called—aptly—Chuck's. I didn't think it was possible to get a truly bad meal anywhere in the Midwest, but Chuck managed to provide it. It was the worst food I had ever had—and remember, I've lived in England. It had all the attributes of chewing-gum, except flavour. Even now when I burp I can taste it.

Afterwards I had a look around the town. There wasn't much. It was mostly just one street, with a grain silo and railroad tracks at one end and my motel at the other, with a couple of gas stations and grocery stores in between. Everyone regarded me with interest. Years ago, in the midst of a vivid and impressionable youth, I read a chilling story by Richard Matheson about a remote hamlet whose inhabitants waited every year for a lone stranger to come to town so that they could roast him for their annual barbecue.

Feeling self-conscious I went into a dark place called Vern's Tap and took a seat at the bar. I was the only customer, apart from an old man in the corner with only one leg. The barmaid was friendly. She wore butterfly eyeglasses and had a beehive hair-do. You could see in an instant that she had been the local good-time girl since about 1931. She had 'Ready for Sex' written all over her face, but 'Better Bring a Paper Bag' written all over her body. Somehow she had managed to pour her capacious backside into some tight red toreador pants and to stretch a clinging blouse over her bosom. She looked as if she had dressed in her granddaughter's clothes by mistake. She was about sixty. It was pretty awful. I could see why the guy with one leg had chosen to sit in the farthest corner.

I asked her what people in Dullard did for fun. 'What exactly did you have in mind, honey?' she said and rolled her eyes suggestively. The 'Ready for Sex' signs flickered, an occurrence I found unsettling. I wasn't used to being hustled by women, though somehow I had always known that when the moment came it would be in some place like downstate Illinois with a sixty-year-old grandmother. I croaked weakly, but once we established that I was only prepared to love her for her mind, she became quite sensible. She told me in great and frank detail about her life, which seemed to have involved a dizzying succession of marriages to guys who were now in prison or dead as a result of shoot-outs, and dropped in breath-takingly candid disclosures like: 'Now Jimmy kilt his mother, I never did know why, but Curtis never kilt nobody except once by accident when he was robbing a gas station and his gun went off. And Floyd—he was my fourth husband—he never kilt nobody neither, but he used to break people's arms if they got him riled.'

'You must have some interesting family reunions,' I ventured politely.

'I don't know what ever became of Floyd,' she went on. 'He had a little cleft in his chin rot year'—after a moment I realized that this was downstate Illinois for 'right here, on this very spot indicated'—'that made him look kind of like Kirk Douglas. He was real cute, but he had a temper on him. I got a two-foot scar right across my back where he cut me with an ice-pick. You wanna see it?' She started to hoist up her blouse, but I stopped her. She went on and on like that for ages. Every once in a while the guy in the corner, who was clearly eavesdropping, would grin, showing large yellow teeth. I expect Floyd had torn his leg off in a moment of high spirits. At the end of our conversation, the barmaid gave me a sideways look, as if I had been slyly trying to fool her and said: 'Say, where do you come from anyway, honey?'

I didn't feel like giving her my whole life story, so I just said, 'Great Britain.'

'Well, I'll tell you one thing, honey,' she said, 'for a foreigner you speak English real good.'

Afterwards I retired with a six-pack to my motel, where I discovered that the bed, judging by its fragrance and shape, had only recently been vacated by a horse. It had a sag in it so severe that I could only see the TV at its foot by splaying my legs to their widest extremity. It was like lying in a wheelbarrow. The night was hot and the air-conditioner, an aged Philco window unit, expended so much energy making a noise like a steelworks that it could only manage to emit the feeblest and most occasional puffs of cool air. I lay with the six-pack on my chest, effectively immobilized, and drank the beers one by one. On the TV was a talk show presided over by some smooth asshole in a blazer whose name I didn't catch. He was the kind of guy for whom personal hair care was clearly a high priority. He exchanged some witless banter with the bandleader, who of course had a silvery goatee, and then turned to the camera and said in a solemn voice: 'But seriously, folks. If you've ever had a personal problem or trouble at work or you just can't seem to get a grip on life, I know you're gonna be real interested in what our first guest has to tell you tonight. Ladies and gentlemen: Dr Joyce Brothers.'

As the band launched into a perky tune and Joyce Brothers strode on-stage, I sat up as far as the bed would allow me and cried: 'Joyce! Joyce Brothers!' as if to an old friend. I couldn't believe it. I hadn't seen Joyce Brothers for years and she hadn't changed a bit. Not one hair on her head had altered a fraction since the last time I saw her, droning on about menstrual flow, in 1962. It was as if they had kept her in a box for twenty-five years. This was as close as I would ever come to time travel. I watched agog as she and Mr Smoothie chattered away about penis envy and fallopian tubes. I kept expecting him to say to her: 'Now seriously, Joyce, here's a question all America has been wanting me to ask you: what sort of drugs do you take to keep yourself looking like that? Also, when are you going to do something about that hair-style? And finally, why is it, do you think, that talk-show bozos like me all over America keep inviting you back again and again?' Because, let's be frank, Joyce Brothers is pretty dull. I mean, if you turn on the Johnny Carson show and she is one of the guests you know that absolutely everybody in town must be at some really big party or première. She is like downstate Illinois made flesh.

Still, like most immensely boring things, there is something wonderfully comforting about her. Her cheery visage on the glowing box at the foot of my bed made me feel strangely warm and whole and at peace with the world. Out here in this crudbucket motel in the middle of a great empty plain I began for the first time to feel at home. I somehow knew that when I awoke I would see this alien land in a new but oddly familiar light. With a happy heart, I fell asleep and dreamt gentle dreams of southern Illinois and the rolling Mississippi River and Dr Joyce Brothers. And it's not often you hear anyone say that either.

Amitav Ghosh

It becomes impossible to ignore the Four Corners once Route 160 enters Colorado's Montezuma County: chevroned signposts spring regularly out of the sand and scrub, urging you towards it. Even if you had never heard of it before, did not know that it is the only point in the USA where four states meet, you are soon curious: it begins to seem like a major station, a Golgotha or Gethsemane, on this well-worn tourist pilgrimage.

The size and sleekness of the trailers and travelling homes heading towards it are eloquent of its significance. These are not the trailers you have grown accustomed to seeing in small towns in the South and Midwest—those shiny aluminium goldfish bowls which sit parked in backyards until the ball game in the next town, when they get hitched on to pick-up trucks and towed out to the ball park to serve as adjuncts for tail-gate parties. Not these; these are no ordinary trailers, they are Recreational Vehicles (RVs)—if not quite palaces, then certainly midtown condos, on wheels.

You only get a real idea of how big they are when you try to pass one on a two-lane road in a Honda Civic which lost its fifth gear 8,000 miles ago. Before you are past the master bedroom, are barely abreast of the breakfast nook, that blind curve that seemed so far away when you decided to make a break for it is suddenly right upon you.

It teaches you respect.

Their owners' imaginations are the only limits on the luxuries those RVs may be made to contain.

Once, on a desolate stretch of road in the deserts of western Utah, I watched an RV pull into a sand-blown Rest Area, right beside my battered Honda Civic. It was almost as long as a supermarket truck and the air around it was sharp with the smell of its newness. A woman with white, curly hair stuck her head out of a window, tried the air, and said something cheerful to someone inside, over the hum of the air-conditioning. A moment later, the door opened, a flight of stairs clicked magically into place under it, and she stepped out, throwing a wave and a cheery 'How you doin'?' in my direction. She was carrying a couple of chairs and a rack of magazines. Her husband climbed out too, and in companionable silence they pulled an awning out of the side of the vehicle and unrolled a ten-foot length of artificial turf under it. She waved again, after the chair, the magazine rack, a pot of geraniums and a vase with an ikebana-ed orchid had been properly arranged on the patch of green. 'I call this my bower,' she said, smiling. 'Join us for cakes and coffee?'

Never had a wilderness seemed so utterly vanquished.

Often those RVs have striking names: Winnebago, Itasca . . . The names of the dispossessed tribes of the Americas hold a peculiar allure for the marketing executives of automobile companies. Pontiac, Cherokee—so many tribes are commemorated in forms of transport. It is not a mere matter of fashion that so many of the cars that flash past on the highways carry those names, breathing them into the air like the inscriptions on prayer wheels. This tradition of naming has a long provenance: did not Kit Carson himself, the scourge of the Navajo, name his favourite horse Apache?

There are many of them on Route 160, those memorials to the first peoples of the Americas, bearing number-plates from places thousands of miles away—New York, Georgia, Alaska, Ontario. Having come this far, everybody wants to see the only point where four states meet.

There cannot be many places in the world quite as beautiful as the stretch of desert, mountain and canyon that sprawls over the borders of the four states of Colorado, Utah, New Mexico and Arizona. For the people who inhabited it at the time of the European conquest—the Diné, who came to be known as the Navajo—it was Diné Bikéyah, the country of the Diné, a land into which the First Beings climbed from the Underworlds through a female reed. To them it was the Fourth World, known as the Glittering.

Route 160 runs through some of the most spectacular parts of the Glittering World: around the caves and canyons of Mesa Verde, and through the spectacular mesas that border on Monument Valley. Curiously, its one dull stretch comes when it dips south of the little town of Cortez and heads towards the Four Corners monument. The landscape turns scraggy and undecided, not quite desert and not quite prairie, knotted with dull grey-green scrub, and scarred by a few shallow ravines and low cliffs.

That is why it is impossible to miss the Four Corners monument.

It springs up out of nowhere, perched atop nothing, framed by the only stretch of dull country in the region. There is nothing remotely picturesque about its surroundings—no buttes, no mesas, not even a salience of rock or an undulation in the plain. With the greatest effort of the imagination it would not be possible to persuade oneself that this may once have been, like so many places in the Glittering World, a haunt of the Spider Woman or the Talking God or the Hero Twins. Legends of that kind need visible metaphors—wind-scarred buttes or lava fields—to attach themselves to the landscape. For the Four Corners monument the landscape does not exist: it sits squatly on the scrub, like a thumb-tack in a map, unbudging in its secular disenchantedness.

There is something majestic and yet uneasy about the absoluteness of its indifference to this landscape and its topography. It is simply a point where two notional straight lines intersect: a line of latitude, thirty-seven degrees North, and a line of longitude, 109 degrees and two minutes West, the thirty-second degree of longitude west of Washington. These two straight lines form the boundaries between the four states. These lines have nothing whatever to do with the Glittering World; their very straightness is testimony to a belief in the unpeopledness of this land—they slice through the *tabula rasa* of the New World leaving it crafted in their own image, enchanted with a new enchantment, the magic of Euclidean geometry.

The centre of the Glittering World was Diné Tah, which lay around Largo Canyon, about eighty miles south-east of the Four Corners monument. To the Navajo it was the sacred heartland of their country. The first time they left it *en masse* was in the 1860s after Colonel Kit Carson and the US Army reduced them to starvation by scorching the earth of their Glittering World. Kit Carson felt no personal animosity towards the Navajo. He is said to have commented once: 'I've seen as much of 'em as any white man livin', and I can't help but pity 'em. They'll all soon be gone anyhow.' He was an unlettered man, given to expressing himself plainly. Unlike him, his commanding officer, General James H. Carleton, had had the benefits of an education. He was therefore able to phrase the matter more dispassionately, clothed in the mellow light of current trends in science and theology: 'In their appointed time He wills that one race of men—as in races of lower animals—shall disappear off the face of the earth and give place to another race . . . The races of the Mammoths and Mastodons, and great Sloths, came and passed away: the Red Man of America is passing away.'

The Navajo were forced to march to an 'experimental' camp at the Bosque Redondo. It was soon clear, however, that the experiment was not going to work, and in 1868 a commission headed by General William T. Sherman was sent to New Mexico to decide what was to be done with the Navajo. Addressing the commission, the Navajo leader, Barboncito, said: 'When the Navajo were first created, four mountains and four rivers were pointed out to us, inside of which we should live, that was to be our country and was given to us by the first woman of the Navajo tribe.' Later, he said to the General: 'I am speaking to you now as if I was speaking to a spirit and I wish you to tell me when you are going to take us to our country.' They were permitted to return later the same year. Of their return, Manuelito, the most renowned of the Navajo war chiefs, said afterwards: 'We felt like talking to the ground, we loved it so.' They were back in Diné Bikéyah, where every butte and mesa pointed to the sacred centre of Diné Tah.

The Four Corners monument evokes a centre too, in its own way. But that central point, the point from which its line of longitude takes its westerly orientation; that central zero degree from which its distance can be so exactly calculated, lies in another landscape, on another continent—far away in Greenwich, England. It is that distant place that the monument unwittingly celebrates.

The monument itself is modest by the standards of monuments in the United States. There is a wide, paved plaza, with plenty of parking space for cars and RVs. On the peripheries there are rows of stalls, manned by people from the neighbouring Ute and Navajo reservations.

In the centre of the plaza is a square cement platform, fenced off by aluminium railings. There is a state flag on each side of the square and towering above them a flag of the United States of America, on an eagle-topped mast. Two straight lines are etched into the cement; they intersect neatly at the centre of the platform. Somebody has thoughtfully provided a small observation post, at one end of the square. There would be little point, after all, in taking pictures of the Four Corners if you couldn't see the two lines intersect. And to get them properly into your frame you have to be above ground level.

You have to queue, both for your turn at the observation post and to get into the centre of the platform. If there are two of you, you have to queue twice at each end, unless you can get somebody to oblige you by taking your picture (and that is easy enough for there are no friendlier people in the world than American tourists). But queuing is no great trial anyway, even in the desert heat, for everyone is good-humoured and it is not long before you find yourself engaged in comparing notes on camp-grounds and motels with everyone around you.

There is a good-natured spirit of competition among the people who walk into the centre of the cement platform: everyone tries to be just a little original when posing for their photographs. A young couple kiss, their lips above the centre and each of their feet in a different state. Another couple pose, more modestly, with one foot on each state and their arms around each others' shoulders. Six middle-aged women distribute themselves between the states, holding hands. An elderly gentleman in Bermuda shorts lets himself slowly down on to his hands and knees and poses with an extremity on each state and his belly-button at the centre. This sets something of a trend; a couple of middle-aged women follow suit. In the end a pretty, teenage girl carries the day by striking a balletic pose on one leg, her toes dead centre on the point where the lines intersect.

Men from the reservations lounge about in the shade of the stalls, around the edges of the plaza. Some rev their cars, huge, lumbering old Chevrolets and Buicks, startling the tourists. A boy, bored, drives into the scrub, sending whirlwinds of sand shooting into the sky. Others sit behind their stalls, selling 'Indian' jewellery and blankets and Navajo Fry Bread. When evening comes and the flow of tourists dwindles, they will pack the contents of their stalls into their cars and go home to their reservations. No one stays the night here; there is nothing to stay for—the attractions of the place are wholly unworldly.

They will be back early next morning: the cars and RVs start arriving soon after dawn, their occupants eager to absorb what they can of the magic of the spectacle of two straight lines intersecting.

HANS MAGNUS
ENZENSBERGER
THE EXTRAVAGANCE
OF THE ITALIANS

Hans Magnus Enzensberger

CUSTOMS DECLARATION. I was relieved when the bill of lading came. The house I had found in the Alban Hills was no noble villa, but my family was small and it would do very well for a year. The lease had been signed; I had been initiated into the secrets of the *carta bollata* (the taxable paper on which Italian legal documents are drawn up); the notary had explained to me the contract's more obscure clauses. Only one small detail was left: my baggage had to be brought through customs.

One morning I went to the appropriate government office, located in an old, seedy, barracks-like building on the outskirts of Rome. I let the taxi driver wait, because I thought it was all a mere formality—no merchandise, no valuables, just a few boxes with household goods, clothes, books. I spent three days of my life in this barracks—in a labyrinth of store-rooms, offices, corridors, ante-chambers and counters—unbelieving at first, then outraged and finally embittered and demoralized. All around me everything was running like clockwork. Brisk, business-like but mysterious people with thick gold watches hurried past me, laughing and exchanging greetings and jokes with the officials. Countless cups of coffee were being drunk. I was the only person who had to wander from one counter to the next with my forms (five copies of each), with duty stamps, clearance vouchers, receipts and certificates. I pleaded my case a dozen times, was forced to wait, was put off with fine words, was sent from pillar to post and was ignored.

On the evening of the third day I received my possessions with a stony expression. There were no fewer than thirty-eight rubber stamps on my bill of lading and my customs declaration. I had fought doggedly and resentfully for each one. That was more than twenty years ago, but even today I'm gripped by an unreasoning repugnance when I catch sight of an Italian customs official.

Of course, I learned long ago that this absurd adventure was my own fault. If I tell my Roman friends about it, they listen with amusement but also with admiration and alarm in their laughter. What? You went there yourself? Alone? They treat me as if I had crossed the Alps on foot. I had broken the basic rules; I had behaved like an American from the Midwest preparing to set up a vegetable stall in the middle of Nepal. I had no idea that if a customs official tried to live off his salary he would be virtually condemned to death by starvation, and that by trying to deal with things on my own I was behaving in a dangerous way. An Italian would never conceive of going through customs by himself. Today I also know who the brisk creatures were who whisked past me in the halls of the customs house. They were the *galoppini*, the professional intermediaries and agents. Pay them and all thirty-eight rubber stamps can be effortlessly mustered in half an hour. Everything works out, everyone makes some money, everyone benefits.

THE BROAD ROAD AND THE NARROW. A foreigner will never understand all the subtleties, but the principle is clear: the direct route is not the direct route. There is no point, under any circumstances, appealing to rights common to everyone. It is more important to acquire a favour, an obligation or a privilege that then demands a deviation, a recommendation, a middleman.

A world of fabulous richness opens up, inexhaustible in its variety. We meet the fireman who always has a ticket for the sold-out performances at La Scala; the neighbour who, a friend of the janitor's daughter, can find out in advance the test questions for the high-school graduation certificate; the Mafia boss who has a teleprinter brought into his cell; the male nurse who obtains a *turno* for a patient—the numbered slip that allows him to attend a clinic for which others have been queueing since six in the morning; the industrialist's wife who hasn't a clue how to mail a registered letter or renew a driving licence, because a crowd of *galoppini*—her husband's secretaries—relieve her of every conceivable errand; and the ironing lady who brings a chicken for this same woman, her employer, because her nephew is a dermatologist to whom the ironing lady now looks to cure her breast cancer (not his speciality), because she is frightened that the obscure, nameless machinery of medicine will kill her . . .

Yet everything has its price. It will take the outsider years to learn the rules of the game. It is easy enough to understand the 50,000-lira note (twenty pounds) placed between the pages of the passport, but what about the visiting card with a couple of friendly, vague lines written to the bursar? The visitor from the north who cries 'Bribery!' makes it too easy for himself. He lacks a feel for suggestion, an ear for words left unspoken. His brutal simplifications don't do justice to the diversity and elegance of the system.

199

What, for example, is the significance of the flowers, strawberries, embroidered napkins and cakes—a whole tableful of offerings—that the wife of a personnel manager, who has moved from Milan to Naples, finds outside her front door the day after her arrival? Who laid all this out? What is the point of this display?

'If you eat even a single cherry from this cake,' she explained to me, 'then you're in their hands. You've concluded an agreement that lasts a lifetime. Not one but three, four, five large families will demand that you get them work, get them into college, get them pensions. What could I do? I had no choice but to go out on to the balcony and proclaim loudly that I didn't need anything, didn't want anything, couldn't accept anything.'

I have no ready answer to the question of how the unwritten laws of Italy relate to the written ones. The country's legal traditions are impressive, its laws numerous and its hair-splitting achievements legendary. There is no shortage of standards, but they are so diverse, complicated and contradictory that only someone tired of life could dream of observing them all. Their strict application would instantly paralyse Italy. You would have to use a magnifying glass to find an Italian citizen living by the book. Anyone who tried to go by the rules, whether applying for a building licence, seeking a residence permit or trying to exchange currency, would suffocate under a paper mountain of files and official documents.

EXTRAS. Every Italian, even the poorest wretch, is privileged. Nobody is a nobody. An observer might conclude that often these privileges exist only in the imagination—but they are the essence of life. A logician might object that a society consisting exclusively of the advantaged, in which each person is 'doing better' than everyone else, is an impossibility. But the Italians have made this miracle—somewhat akin to the Indian rope trick or squaring the circle—come to pass.

Five long-distance lorry drivers stand at a bar in Andria, and each one asks for a coffee: one wants it *molto stretto* (extra strong), another *macchiato* (with just a dash of milk), the next one *con latte caldo* (with warm milk), his colleague asks for *cappuccino,* but the last one calls triumphantly through the bar: '*Un espresso doppio con latte aparte!'* (a double espresso with the milk on the side). He's known in every truck-stop from Verona to Brindisi, and no bar-keeper would dare deny him his desire. He's not average, he's special. The round of privileges begins harmlessly but it continues endlessly.

A N EXTREMIST. He says: 'We hate equality. We despise it. We only like distinctions. Communism in Italy is a joke. Even the word "comrade" is hyperbole. We aren't a collective; we're an accumulation of free individuals. We loathe anonymity. No one feels responsible for the "whole", everyone looks out for himself, for his clan, his clique, his gang. Of course, that means we feel contempt for our neighbours; we dump our garbage on other people's doorsteps. There were two murders in our town this summer because noise had become unbearable in the heat. One was right next door. For nights on end the whole street couldn't sleep, so one guy drew his gun and shot another who was making a racket. That's normal. No one has a conscience about anything. We have left-wing rhetoric but no social super-ego. We don't need any good shepherds, pastors or wardens. Too bad for you, you'll say. Maybe you're right. But I also think there's something healthy in all of this.'

A TTEMPTS AT EXPLANATION. HYPOTHESES. EXCUSES. It's an old story, a very old story. It's a consequence of the late unification of Italy. It's related to the fact that the state always appeared as an occupying power, so the people resisted it. It's the Mediterranean character, like the Spanish or the Levantine or the Greek. It's a matter of capitalist attitudes, remnants of feudalism. It's a rejection of the 'naked cash nexus' Marx talks about, of the impersonal power of money that forces an empty and faceless equality on people. It's due to the traditional structure of the family, as it fought for survival in agrarian conditions. It's a sign of our backwardness . . .

No, someone says, it's none of these things. I'll tell you what's to blame: particularism, localism. There are no Italians in Italy, only natives and newcomers. As in art history, everyone defines himself by where he was born: *il Parmegiano, il Veronese, il Perugino.* And that's how it stays. The man from Turin remains the man from Turin, even if he has been living in Cagliari for a generation. That explains why he's so down-to-earth and meticulous and why he understands nothing about Sardinia. The poor soul doesn't have a clue! The Milanese woman born in Giglio has to invite, put up and protect anyone who comes from Giglio, even if she left the island forty years ago, even if she returns only at Easter to visit her aged mother. Giglio will always be her capital, her metropolis. On the other hand, she can't be held responsible for Milan. Her distinction is to have come into the world in this spot and nowhere else. One may admire other villages, regions, countries, continents—but envy? Or even love? Never! So every Italian town is the best, with perhaps one exception, on which everyone agrees. The exception, and I don't know why, is Rovigo. ('Oh, you're from Rovigo? What a shame.')

A N EXTREMIST (CONTINUED). He says: 'Where does your equality get you? Of all the slogans of 1789, it's the emptiest. Your equality is a phantom. It has never come remotely close to being realized. Or do you think there's anything in the so-called socialist countries deserving of the name? What's the situation at home, in the decent, well-protected, orderly north? Is there no selfishness, no muddle, no nepotism, no corruption, no privilege?

'I know your objection. You'll fall back on the formal equality of citizens and praise it to the skies. Equality before the law; the fact that even the rich pay taxes; the conviction that you have certain rights, just like everyone else, to which you are entitled without a letter of recommendation, without patronage, without a *galoppino*, "without respect of person". Maybe you will extol the joys of anonymity, the impersonal exchange of services, commodities, ideas, jobs and administrative documents. You'll tell me that alienation is a pleasure, that inconspicuousness is a release, that you live in the best of all possible worlds—a social machine that functions smoothly.

'To me you're like millionaires who don't want to admit they're millionaires, who travel second-class and run around in shabby jackets, enjoying their privileges in secret because they're ashamed of them. When it's a matter of life and death, then everybody, even in Frankfurt and Stockholm, wants the best doctor and the most

202

expensive private hospital—but discreetly, of course. The radical English trade union boss sends his children to the public school whose abolition he champions. The truth is, you can't bear the truth! Your social-democratic utopias, your Swedish dream in which naked power dresses up in angelic white, are bleak and dreary.'

THE POTENTATES. No important figure in Italy can be accused of resorting to such disguise. Power, the ultimate privilege, isn't hidden. Invoked and exhibited, displayed and admired, it's an inexhaustible topic of conversation. Its transformation, its nuances and its vicissitudes are discussed with passion. No one is interested in structural, impersonal or distant forms of the exercise of power. Power is experienced as real, and taken seriously, only when embodied in a person or encountered face to face. One can— one wants to—touch it; something of its *mana*, its electricity, is transferred to anyone who comes in contact with it. It's the most widely used aphrodisiac. In the word *potenza* the political significance merges with the sexual. A famous Sicilian saying expresses this duality with matchless precision: '*Commandare e meglio di fottere*' (Ruling is better than fucking).

THE DREAM. I'm sitting on a high, old-fashioned, black-leather barber's chair, which is being cranked further and further back till I'm almost lying horizontal. In the tall, peeling mirors I see only familiar faces—the men from the village, sitting on a long wooden bench and waiting: the tobacconist, the priest, the wine-grower, the man from the petrol station. They talk, they leaf through the newspaper, they smoke. Outside, dogs doze on the piazza in the midday heat. The barber, a toothless old man, has just lathered me. The clock on the wall says a minute before noon.

Then the door opens and a bald little gentleman enters. A freshly and carefully pressed brown suit, medal ribbons in his buttonhole, a watch-chain, pointed shoes brilliantly polished. He stands still and looks around. All conversation ceases. The barber rushes over to the new customer and greets him with enthusiasm. Astonished, I watch as the tobacconist takes his hat, the priest helps him off with his jacket and the petrol station attendant hands him his newspaper. The fat man doesn't say a word. He only runs his long, pink tongue over his lips and solemnly sits down on the chair beside me. He's quickly rubbed with eau-de-Cologne, tucked up in hot and cold cloths, massaged, powdered, combed. No one bothers about me; I feel the soap slowly drying on my cheeks. I'd like to stand up and protest, but I can't rise from my chair. It's hot. I hear the scraping of the blade, the smacking of fingers on the fat man's skin. A long time passes. Then the fat man jumps up and everyone thanks him. He doesn't leave a tip; in fact, he doesn't pay at all, but the barber's apprentice kisses his hand. I stare at him with utter loathing because I've realized at last who this is before me—this puffed-up zero, this fat little man, is 'power'.

Hardly has the door closed behind him than they all laugh and slap their thighs, pick up newspapers and light their cigarettes again. 'And why doesn't he pay?' I ask. 'Why doesn't he wait until it's his turn, like everyone else?'

The apprentice looks at me with astonishment. 'But he comes here every day at twelve on the dot for his shave,' says the old barber.

'Why do you put up with it?' I cry angrily.

'It's none of your business,' says the tobacconist.

'We'll do what we like,' says the priest.

'Damn foreigner,' mutters the petrol station attendant.

I jump up and run out of the shop. Suddenly I'm standing in the middle of the street in Milan, opposite San Babila, with the village barber's white bib around my neck. Traffic racing past. A little boy points at me; others turn around and laugh. There's still soap on my face.

THE COINS. Chewing-gum in your pockets, nothing but chewing-gum. Does the under-secretary of state still remember? Do my dear friends still remember?

Of course not. They shrug their shoulders. It is as if I had asked about King Zog of Albania or the slogan *Tunis-Corsica-Djibouti*, which a couple of million Italians got worked up about at the end of 1938: total amnesia. And yet the great small-change crisis, the epoch of chewing-gum and soup cubes, is only nine, seven, five years ago. The city of Róme, with its 2,200-year history of coinage, the country to which Europe owes the invention of double-entry book-keeping, collateral loans and credit, balances and discounts, premiums and balance sheets. Even the word 'bank' comes from the Italian. Yet after the greatest boom in its history, richer than ever before, this country, the eighth-largest industrial power in the world, was no longer capable of supplying its inhabitants with those round pieces of metal that have always been essential for the simplest everyday transactions. In those days, anyone in Italy who wanted to make a phone call, buy a couple of tomatoes, drink a cup of coffee or mail a letter had to be ready to accept caramels for change. And it wasn't just for a couple of weeks because of a metal-workers' strike, or for three months because the mint had burned down—chewing-gum was legal tender in Italy for five whole years, from AD 1975 to AD 1979, just as cowrie shells once were in the South Pacific and Africa.

In Switzerland, where the national currency is guarded like the Holy Grail, the government would have been brought down within a week. In Japan the minister responsible would have committed seppuku. Even in the sluggish Soviet Union a couple of heads might have rolled. In Italy governments presided over the débâcle without losing a moment's sleep. The only people at their wits' end were the tourists. The natives responded with stoic patience and nimble improvisation. After just a few months, the country hit upon a magical solution. The Italians let the Finance Ministry go on snoring and printed their own money. A new world, that of the mini-cheque, came into being.

Immediately millions of little scraps of paper in every colour flooded into the cash registers. The face value of these cheques is said to have amounted to thirty or 100 or 300 billion lire; every expert names a different figure. And it hardly matters whether an estimate is out by a factor of ten, for of course there was no trace of control over this national game of Monopoly.

Whenever there's an element of doubt, the bank always wins such parlour games, but if the whole thing is to work, ordinary players must have a chance too. I enter the bank and deposit a few million lire in cash in my account. After all, there are still enough banknotes available—the printing presses are working tirelessly. In return the bank gives me huge quantities of mini-cheques, printed on blotting paper, in units of fifty or 100 lire. I put this small change into circulation in the shop, in the payroll, at the ticket office and in

the restaurant. The bank is satisfied. It can work with the money
I've deposited in a non-interest-bearing account. A fine piece of
business. My cheques circulate. They're torn, forgotten, thrown
away. Perhaps two-thirds are redeemed, perhaps only half. It would
be impossible to find out exactly how many, because who is going to
insist on careful book-keeping in such chaotic conditions? After a
couple of years I go to the bank and ask how much money is in my
account. Strictly speaking, no one knows. But somehow we'll
manage to reach an agreement. The easiest thing is simply to split
the spoils—I and the bank, the bank and I. During the play-money
years, not only did all the country's financial institutions operate
according to this system, but so did the co-operatives, the
department stores, the highway administrations, the newsagents,
the nationalized enterprises and the chambers of commerce—as
well as, presumably, a fair number of bankrupts and bogus
companies.

I recall that, on a night flight over Asia, I met an Italian-
American banker working for the International Monetary
Fund. In the dim light—the other passengers had curled up and
were asleep—the pale, gaunt, loquacious Genoese, who couldn't
stop fidgeting, explained the importance of the Italian billions to
me.

'Utterly absurd! The mini-cheques are a preposterous way of
expanding credit, and they have an inflationary effect too, that's
obvious. But my countrymen—please don't quote me—like
inflation. They complain about it, but you mustn't pay attention to
their complaints. The more zeros the better. Anyone can become a
millionaire. Other countries would have revalued long ago, at a
hundred or a thousand to one. But in Rome the so-called *lira
pesante*, a lira that would be worth something, doesn't have a
chance. That would smack of austerity, of restrictions, of doing
without! But inflation—that's the miracle of the loaves and fishes,
the solution of economic problems by magic. It's an irresistible
temptation! The truth is, we're living beyond our means and have
been for twenty years.'

'An admirable characteristic,' I said. 'You're just very
generous people. Luxury, the good life, where else in Europe can
you still find them? Only in Italy . . .'

'Nonsense. It's nothing but vanity. In Italy extravagance is not a national mania, it's a social compulsion. The cars are always a little too large, the restaurant bills always go into the hundred thousands. We're all beggars wanting to play at being lords.'

'But the level of savings,' I objected. 'More than twelve per cent of income! Higher than the Japanese! How do you manage to throw your money out of the window and save it at the same time?'

'By the ultimate trick, by the magic of multiplication: inflation! The disappearance of metal money is no more than this operation's physical expression. Metal is annoying, it's too hard, too palpable; it has to be dissolved; it becomes blotting paper, chewing-gum, the little piece of chocolate that melts in your pocket . . . And what's best of all is that no one's surprised, no one's worried, no one gets excited.'

No one? On the contrary! I remember years of embittered 'discussion', commentaries, parliamentary debates, protests, revelations, editorials, appeals. The small-change scandal was a wonderful opportunity for quarrelling, an ideal hotbed of rumours, theories and jokes. In the fall of 1976, a judge in Perugia ordered the seizure of all the mini-cheques in Italy—an action that, if carried out, would have kept the Italian police busy for months. Later a judge in Milan quashed the order with an even more ingenious justification. The assistant state secretary in charge of the matter, a dentist from Vicenza, explained to Parliament:

> With reference to the legality of the mini-cheques . . . um, um . . . The government has, well, always taken a negative position. There are anomalies in their issue . . . mm, mm . . . which, at least in the material sense . . . [scrape, scrape] . . . represent a clear infringement of current regulations in the area of circulation of cheques. Ahem. Inasmuch as these can in no way serve de facto as substitutes for cash.

This rhetorical gem indicates rather precisely the course the government intended to take—that is, dull-witted denial of the facts. The public, meanwhile, displayed a quite alarming adaptability. To cope with the shortage of small change, the retail trade simply rounded off its prices to the nearest zero. On the black

207

market, legal coins were traded with a mark-up of ten to fifteen per cent. Of course, that meant that the few coins still remaining were hoarded systematically. Public transportation was an especially good source of revenue for the black market. When the company running Venice's buses and *vaporetti* ordered its employees to hand over the change they had taken in, rather than sell it, the conductors threatened to strike.

But how did it all happen? Had the Italians gone mad? Had they forgotten the art of punching out round pieces of metal and putting inscriptions on them? I assembled a small collection of the most popular explanations, which I can now pass on to the reader:

1. 'There was no metal left' (bank employee, Venice, 1977).
2. 'In Japan and Singapore they made buttons out of our fifty-lira pieces, and that's why the coins disappeared' (theatre critic, Rome, 1983).
3. 'It's the trade unions' fault. They've ruined the whole country with their demands. That's why the mint doesn't work either' (taxi driver, Milan, 1976).
4. 'The foreigners who came for Holy Year took away our small change as souvenirs' (the finance minister of the Italian Republic, 1975).
5. 'It's a conspiracy by the banks, which are making a huge profit at the expense of the little man' (Communist trade unionist, 1977).
6. 'Coins cost too much, and Parliament didn't want to pay' (assistant in shoe shop, Como, 1983).
7. 'The 100-lira pieces were taken to Switzerland in huge trucks, and the companies there made watch-cases out of them' (*La Stampa*, 1976).
8. 'The coins are just stuck in the vending machines, which aren't emptied often enough' (waiter, Naples, 1976).
9. 'In the mint's present facility it is impossible either to increase production adequately or to guarantee minimum conditions for the health and safety of the work-force' (Senate Committee for Finance and

Treasury Affairs, 1976).
10. 'What do you expect? That's just how we are . . .
    Siamo negati per queste cose (We're hopeless at
    things like that). You can't do anything about it. It's
    all a mess, *un paese di merda* (a shitty country) . . .
    All these politicians and civil servants from the
    south. Actually, it was a mistake to throw out the
    Austrians' (*vox populi*, 1975–1983).

Three things about these remarkable explanations: first, they
are, without exception, wrong. Second, they all completely ignore
the state of affairs they're supposed to explain. Only one, that of the
Senate Committee, says anything about the mint's operation. And
third, they're evidence of an imagination untroubled by facts. They
tend towards either anecdote or abstraction, but in every case
towards mythomania. A degree of paranoia is evident in most of
these stories. Dark, anonymous forces ('the system', 'the banks',
'the trade unions', 'the civil servants from the south'—i.e., the
Mafia) are made responsible for the small-change crisis, or else it's
the greedy tourists, the evil Swiss, the inscrutable Malays, the slant-
eyed Japanese, who have taken the hard-earned 100-lira coins away
from the Italians.

The dull reality, of course, was quite different. Devoid of any
such secrets and conspiracies, it centred upon the obvious question:
how is it possible to strike more coins? There was no getting around
the issue. There was also nothing new about it; the problem had
been foreseen for decades. All that was needed were a few readily
available figures, a sheet of paper and a pencil. In the industrialized
countries coins averaged around eight per cent of the money in
circulation (six per cent in the Federal Republic of Germany, eight
per cent in Great Britain, 10.5 per cent in the United States). In
Italy the percentage had sunk first to three per cent then to 1.8 and
finally to 1.2 per cent. The catastrophe was entirely predictable.
Only the 'political forces', blind as moles but lacking the energy and
instincts of those remarkable animals, were incapable of such an
analysis.

In the faraway year of 1968 it had nevertheless dawned on an
unknown civil servant; a faint suspicion had arisen in him and he
had drawn up a bill. A new mint! Why not? said the MPs, and

agreed to make three billion lire available for this worthy purpose. Then for eight years nothing happened. In 1976 a further twelve billion was voted for the phantom new mint, and the municipal administration of Rome adopted a new development plan. A piece of land was found on the Via di Grotta Gregna in the eastern part of the city. And in Parliament an under-secretary (not a dentist this time) declared, 'We shall now be in a position, taking into account all the limitations I have mentioned, to undertake an examination of the plan for building a new mint.'

And there the matter rests: with the examination, the limitations, and a plan gathering dust in the drawers of some ministry or other.

TYPICALLY ITALIAN. Which is it, then? The opera or the Mafia? A *cappuccino* or bribery? Macchiavelli or Missoni? Whenever anyone says that something or other is 'typically Italian', I want to jump up with impatience, overturn my chair and run out of the room. Could anything be more barren than the study of 'national psychology', that mouldy garbage heap of stereotypes, prejudices and accepted ideas? And yet it is impossible to dislodge these traditional garden gnomes with their naïvely painted faces: the taciturn Scandinavian, blonder than straw; the obstinate German, beer stein in hand; the red-faced, garrulous Irishman, always smelling of whiskey; and, of course, the Italian with his moustache, forever sensual but regrettably unreliable, brilliant but lazy, passionate but scheming . . .

The notion of the typical also seems to be indispensable for home consumption, for the elevated purpose of self-criticism—a genre to which Italian authors have made outstanding contributions. In Alberto Arbasino's furious diatribe *Un paese senza*, one can read: 'It must be recognized that regardless of every kind of survey technique, behavioural pattern or grid, an ancient, archetypal, and cunning meanness predominates in the behaviour of the Italian . . . The anomalies, monstrosities, madness and outrageous crimes of contemporary Italy—yes, even the 'typically Italian' horror stories—can hardly be said to be anomalous, monstrous or shocking when considered in their "normal" context.' How did Arbasino's countrymen respond to these 350 pages of

210

merciless abuse? They elected the author to Parliament three years later!

B ut the unsuspecting foreigners, on the other hand! As long as a handbag isn't actually snatched or a car broken into, their enthusiasm remains unbounded. Take Gisela G., for example, an unemployed teacher from Munster in Westphalia. She has retired to taste the joys of solitude, i.e., to the obligatory farmhouse in Tuscany. A couple of drop-outs from Dusseldorf—former marketing experts—have built an extension on to the nineteenth-century villa on the hill. A commune of hippies from Berlin is living in the old school building amid empty wine bottles and dirty dishes. A mysteriously named 'Study Group for Transpersonal Therapy' has installed itself a few doors down; for a weekend fee of 600 marks (£200), tired branch managers and sports-writers can re-arm themselves for the struggle for survival in Frankfurt. And a Swiss photographer is said recently to have bought the manor on the other side of the river.

Anyway, Gisela G. writes to me (and I have no idea how to reply):

> Dear M.,
>
> I feel sorry for you! I don't know you can bear to go on living in those 'well-ordered' German surroundings. I've been unable to cope with them for a long time now. In the north we're constantly being terrorized—by money, by technology, by discipline. Too much property, too many neuroses. Life here is simpler, more natural, more human, not so anonymous and cold and not just because of the climate. I look after the garden, I meet the people from the village on the piazza . . . I'm simply happier here.

Good for you, dear Gisela! Best of luck. It's just that your ingenuous letter is completely plagiarized, a compendium of platitudes that have figured in European literature for 200 years . . . Your Tuscan idyll is nothing but a feeble recapitulation. A great love for Italy was first kindled in the sensitive natures of certain visitors in the middle of the eighteenth century. Since then it's become the basis of a billion-dollar industry. It has remained an unrequited love from the start. No Italian would dream of moving voluntarily to Munster in Westphalia or to Trelleborg or the Hook of Holland without a compelling practical reason.

At home, dear Gisela, you were always getting worked up about acid rain and the arms race—but in Tuscany you wear rose-coloured glasses. Or haven't you noticed that the Italians don't give a damn about the environment and think pacifism is a fad? You complain about the wealth and greed of the north—but what would you do if the monthly cheque from the cold north stopped coming and you had to earn a living in Poggibonsi? The local people are friendly as long as you can pay. They tolerate you, just as the whole country accepts the permanent invasion from the north, and I admire their patience. I don't find it surprising that they pluck you clean as a Christmas goose, charmingly, ruthlessly and with an irony that escapes you entirely.

In fact, I understand you all too well, because I share your stubborn love of Italy. We can't survive without this refuge. It's our favourite projection, our drive-in movie theatre, our all-purpose Arcadia. Now, as 200 years ago, we can compensate for our defects here, load up with illusions and dig among the ruins of an ancient, half-forgotten utopia.

Have it your own way. But why must this love be so ignorant, stupid and narrow-minded? Why does Gisela so persistently overlook everything in Italy that cries to heaven? If she came home to cool, boring Munsterland and found conditions there like those in Mestre or Avellino, she would be outraged by so much cruelty, harshness and indifference to others.

Every doting love has its reverse side. Tourism can't exist without a double standard. When the visitor from the north has spent his last lira and returned to the German, Belgian or Swedish autumn, doesn't he after all heave a secret sigh of relief because everything in the north—the central heating, the state, the telephone—works so well? Then when he opens his newspaper and reads the latest horror stories from Italy (chaos, Camorra, corruption) he leans back and thinks, *It can't happen here*. And this pious belief is the final proof that he hasn't understood anything.

Translated from the German by Martin Chalmers

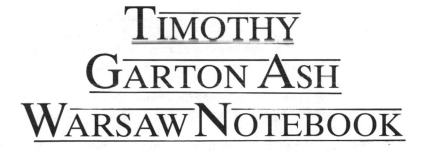

A.M. for ZL?' says my tattered Polish notebook, in a deliberately illegible scrawl. 'Berlin-Berdayev.' 'Lordly invite for K.B. & E.K.?' And beside another scrawled initial: 'Where unpublished novel "The Heritage"?'

During the war, Jurek had another name, false identity papers and a beard. As we talked, a short-wave receiver crackled on the police wavelengths. Mozart for conspirators.

If you want to transport samizdat you must strengthen the rear springs. Otherwise the pigs will notice the headlamps' high beam.

'Why are they chanting "Gestapo"?' asks an elderly bystander at the demonstration. 'It should be "SS".'

Underground groups are called 'structures'. Some people offer friends the service of their 'structures'. This makes them important. Then it turns out the structures don't exist. Such men are 'structuralists'.

I flew in from London the day Felek came out of hiding. After two years. 'We're waiting for the police,' they said. We drank. We listened to ancient music. Bob Dylan. Pink Floyd. Felek and Spot swapped tales from internment, conspiracy, occupation: this one, the last, the last but two. We waited. And I watched the pretty, bright-eyed daughter, strangely trembling. For Daddy had come home from the war.

I flew British Airways: just two and a half hours from peace to war. Departure: 1983. Arrival: 1945.

'She'll eat her words,' says the English phrase. And so she did. Mind you, they were written on cigarette paper. We sat on the park bench. She read off the cryptic message. Then she popped it into her mouth. Just like that. Mmmm, finger-licking good. Care for another?

At home you never say anything important. You write it down. Names particularly. Then you burn the paper in the candle. Unless you're hungry, of course.

Underground publishers of my acquaintance thought they had a police spy in the firm. So they sent to him a pretty girl. With a mission. She made love to him. He confessed to her. He is no longer a publisher. As was said of a lady in the Maquis: *'Elle a couché pour la France.'*

Here's a brilliant new writer: Dawid Warszawski. Let's profile him on the features page. Let's get him writing for *Granta*. Except that nobody knows who he is. The pseudonym is inviolate. Early in the war, he tells me, he received a letter from a group of professors via one of the samizdat journals. They admired his writing. They would like to meet him in person. He replied, by the same circuitous route, that this was alas impossible 'for conspiratorial reasons'. Back came a frosty little note from the professors. They couldn't understand what he was talking about, they wrote, since they had already met Dawid Warszawski, not once but several times. These conversations had been most stimulating. Somewhere out there was a prize structuralist. Or a laughing policeman.

A cat jumps on to my lap. His name? 'Offset'. A kitten of martial law, when his owners' dream was an offset machine for producing samizdat.

Laughing matter. Yet this war had real victims too. There are fresh graves in the Powazki.

Now 1988 was a 'watershed year', 'a year of peace', they tell us. The Cold War has ended. The division of Europe will be overcome. The eagle shall lie down with the bear and all will be well and all manner of things will be well.

I read it in the newspapers so it must be true. But I shall believe it

when cigarette papers are for rolling cigarettes
when kittens are called Figaro and radios are for Mozart
when ZL can be there and A.M. here
when my notebook has only real names and full addresses.

T he twenty-seventh of August, 1984. We're in Empangeni's courthouse, a single-storey brick building next door to the post office. Mr Justice John Broome, presiding, is a dignified eminence. His manner is ascetic, his language grave and precise. Glenda Sanders, counsel for the defence, is young, blond and ambitious. She has a Cambridge degree behind her and a job with a major American law firm in her near future. The prosecutor, Dorian Paver, assistant attorney-general, is a graduate of the liberal University of Cape Town. Save for the interpreter, the officers of the court are all white.

It's not just their skins that are white; their minds are white, too. They are generic whites with western values. They are all of the same high caste; all speak an English devoid of the flat, angular vowels of the white South African commoner. The ritual of justice about to be enacted is white, western, ancient and alien. It has nothing to do with Africa.

Africa is outside. You can hear it through the open windows— a clamouring throng of several hundred Zulus held at bay by cops with dogs. They're climbing trees and standing on one another's shoulders to catch a glimpse of their hero of the moment, the captured Hammerman.

Simon Mpungose is thirty-five, solid, chunky, muscular. His skin is smooth, brown and shining. He has a neat moustache. He's wearing a short-sleeved white sports shirt, white slacks and ankle shackles. His dark eyes are full of humour and intelligence, and, when he smiles, there is something truly charismatic about him.

Simon smiles a great deal. Since the trial opened this morning, in fact, he's done little but smile and laugh. Simon is on trial for his life, but he seems very happy. His fellow Zulus reach for words meaning 'full', 'ecstatic' or even 'transfigured' to describe the state he is in. He has fulfilled his destiny; he is ready to die.

He has refused to mount a defence. The moment Judge Broome gavelled the court to order, Simon demanded that the trial be aborted. He had committed the murders, he said, and that was that. He wanted to be taken away and hanged. The ritual of white justice had to take its course, however, so Judge Broome ordered him to sit down and shut up. Simon responded by instructing his counsel not to challenge the state's case in any way. And then he sat back, smiling sympathetically, while a parade of state witnesses told their stories.

The gist of the state's case is that the accused is a common criminal. Dorian Paver contends that Simon broke into white homes because he wanted a gun and killed their sleeping inhabitants for fear that they'd wake up and catch him. It isn't really necessary for Paver to establish a clear motive, however, because the accused admits everything. Indeed, the prosecutor's most serious problem is to make himself heard above the din of Africa, above the constant hubbub coming in through the windows.

Even Judge Broome finds it trying. 'I don't like people peering through the windows,' he says at one point. 'It is unsettling and objectionable.'

Paver plods on, laying out his case. There is the story of Wendy Trollip, who woke up in a bed drenched with blood. There is the story of Debbie and Bennie Good, who woke up in intensive care. There is the story of the Magaskills, who didn't wake up at all. And, finally, there is the testimony of Dave Brauteseth, who tells of the morning he discovered Justin and Terri Smith dead in their bedroom. On that note the state closes its case, and it is Simon's turn.

He shuffles out of the dock in his leg-irons and takes up his position in the witness-box. He lays his hand on the Bible and swears to tell the truth. The Zulu interpreter, a black man in a pinstriped suit, stands beside him, and Simon starts speaking. His voice is pitched oddly high for a man of his bulk. He talks Zulu, but his words emerge in the curiously Victorian English of the interpreter.

At the outset, Glenda Sanders asks a few questions, but Simon doesn't want to be led. He knows he is doomed and that these are his last public words. So he wants to talk to the judge, man to man. He wants to tell the judge what it is to be black in South Africa.

'Everything that is happening today,' he says, 'I have seen it before; I saw it in my dream in the prison at Barberton.'

In many ways, the Hammerman's tale was the tale of a black Everyman. Simon was a Zulu. His tribe was broken by whites in 1879 and stripped of its best lands. The Zulus were ground down by the British and ground down still further by the apartheid policies of D.F. Malan, who came to power in the year of Simon's birth. Subjugation was his birthright, and oppression awaited him.

During the years in which Simon should have been in school, South Africa was ruled by Dr Hendrik Verwoerd, a blatant racist who openly opposed education for blacks. They were destined to wield shovels, he argued, so why teach them to read and encourage them to imagine that they might be allowed to enter 'the green pastures' of civilized life? So Simon never set foot inside a school. His mother died when he was young, and he was farmed out to relatives who didn't want him and treated him cruelly. By the age of twelve, he was labouring in the cane fields on nearby white farms or washing dishes in farmers' kitchens. The money he earned was never enough to live on, so he got into trouble for pilfering. He ran away with a friend and lived in the bush outside a big city. The South African state made no real provision for such children. Simon's juvenile criminal record was pathetic and left no doubt about his desperation. On one occasion, he was punished for stealing ten cents; on several others, for stealing food.

In his late teens, Simon came up before a white magistrate who took a look at his lengthening record and decided to put an end to his nonsense. Simon had no lawyer. The state provided a defence for indigent blacks only in capital cases. He was illiterate and could barely speak English. He wanted to tell the court that he stole only because he was hungry. He wanted to say that he had never harmed anyone or used violence, but he wasn't asked to explain himself. He was just another larcenous Kaffir, so the magistrate sent him to prison for seven years. 'I felt,' Simon said later, 'that they slammed the door on me and wrote *closed* upon it.' He tried to hang himself, but the rope snapped, and he found himself sitting on the floor of his isolation cell, feeling more desolate than ever. It was the first of many suicide attempts. Next, he launched a suicidal escape attempt, hoping to be shot in the course of it. He got away unharmed. When the police picked him up again, however, his sentence was lengthened, and he was sent to a prison farm called Barberton.

On the day Simon arrived, he received the traditional Barberton welcome. A white lieutenant explained the brutal verities of life. 'The train does not go past Barberton,' he told Simon. 'There is no turning back. Here, even the human brain changes. There are only two ways here. It is death or living. Don't think of anything; just crack the stones. There must be no other thoughts for you if you want to live.' And then a throng of white warders and black trusties closed in on the boy and broke him in, whipping and kicking him. He could not walk for a month.

In Barberton, convicts broke rocks in the sun under the guns of white warders. Discipline was ruthless. Prisoners who stepped out of line were whipped so mercilessly that the blood had to be washed out of their cells with hoses. Simon once saw white warders ironing the body of a black convict they had beaten to death. They were trying to erase the welts on the corpse, to avoid troublesome questions. 'It came to a point,' Simon told his judge, 'where it ceased in me that I fear a white person. And I also lost love of him.' The rocks Simon smashed with his hammer were white. 'It is not long,' he said, 'before the rocks are the white man's head.'

In Barberton, Simon was visited by a prophetic dream. 'The dream was like a voice from the gods,' he said, 'a messenger I should not deny.' In this dream, he started swelling and bloating, growing taller and taller. He flexed his muscles, and the prison walls crumbled around him. The white police opened fire, but their bullets passed right through him. He crushed them like insects and then rolled away across the landscape like a thunderstorm, obliterating all the whites who stood in his path.

In that state, Simon encountered a figure of overwhelming power. 'This man,' he said, 'this person, my persecutor, did not have a face, but his head looked just like the rocks that I broke with my hammer. It is easy for those round white rocks to take the shape of a head. So I killed him. And when I had killed him, they took me away and I was small again, and they put me to death and I had

221

freedom from torment.'

A Zulu cannot ignore such a dream, even if he calls himself a Christian. Such a dream reveals a man's *isipiwo*, his destiny. Simon prayed to his Christian God to be freed from the destiny his dream revealed. Many years passed, but the dream remained strong in his heart. In 1983 the prison authorities informed him that he was about to be paroled. Upon hearing the news, Simon asked for an interview with the prison commandant. He asked if the major could arrange to have him deported from South Africa. Simon even asked if the major could keep him in prison, because he was full of rage and feared he would kill if set free in South Africa. But the white commandant just laughed at him and said, 'Go away from here. You are mad.' And so, in July 1983, Simon Mpungose was given fifteen rand, an ill-fitting suit, a cardboard suitcase containing two shirts and underpants, and a train ticket home to Empangeni.

Simon had been in prison seventeen years. A free man at last, he trudged into the hills, to the village where he had been born. There was nothing left of it, or so he said, save a cluster of tombstones. Simon's entire family was dead, or so he said. So he walked back to Ngwelezane, where people had little to spare for him save sympathy. He was alone in the world. He had no money, no food, and nowhere to stay. He felt, he said, 'like a just-born baby'. He didn't even have a pass, so he had no right to work or even to be in Ngwelezane.

South African blacks hated the pass and the serfdom it symbolized. Even so, it was not easy to get one. To get a pass, you had to step onto an infuriating bureaucratic treadmill manned by scornful and obstructive clerks. You had to stand in the sun all day outside the Administration Bureau, waiting your turn at the counter. When Simon finally reached the head of the line, the clerk said, 'Where's your photograph? You must have a photograph.' But a photo cost three rand, and Simon had less than half that in his pocket. He begged the balance, had his 'snap' taken, and returned to the endless line.

This time, the clerk behind the counter wanted to see the signature of Simon's tribal chief, granting permission to leave his district. Simon's chief had three kraals, three far-flung homesteads out in the reserve. It would have taken days of walking to visit them all. So Simon begged for an exemption, and the clerk grudgingly granted him a 'duplicate', a temporary pass.

Pass in hand, he trudged the streets until he landed a job as a labourer on a construction site. The work was hard and the wages low. 'Yes, I wanted money,' he said. 'No, not to be rich. All I wanted was enough to live on, like the other people of means.' So he complained to his white boss. 'I told the white man how much my travelling expenses were,' he said, 'and how much the food cost me. It was too little to live on. When I told the white man so, I noticed his face, how it changed. He told me in Afrikaans that he was not happy with what I had stated to him. His face also told me this.' The white man snatched Simon's hard-won pass and tore it to pieces before his eyes. 'Now try and find work,' he snapped.

'In this world,' Simon said later, 'sometimes the little things change to a big thing.' That white man's act, such a commonplace act of white cruelty and contempt, changed into a very big thing indeed. It was a crime to deface a passbook, but when Simon reported the matter to the police, they just shrugged. So he trudged into town to report it to the white municipality, which referred him to the Administration Board, which referred him back to the police, who laughed at him.

And so Simon was back on square one. He was thirty-four years old and still had nothing—no pass, no home, and no money in his pocket. He couldn't face the thought of returning to the lines outside the pass office and then pounding the streets in search of a job he might never find. 'There were lots of people looking for work,' he said. 'So I laughed with myself. I have been trying to live a decent life and be a good citizen, but from what I have discovered, it means I am an outcast.' He thought deeply about his plight and decided he had had enough. 'I saw there was no point in running away from it,' he said. 'I saw there was no other way but to follow the swallows.'

To follow the swallows is a Zulu proverb that means to die, but what do white judges and lawyers know of such things? It would only have confused them. So the interpreter said that Simon decided 'to start another type of life' and left it at that.

Simon's next statement was rooted in an even more obscure Zulu metaphor, the metaphor of the furrow that carries the waters of life. Simon spoke of labouring to open the furrow so that the waters might flow in behind him and bear him away, but white men knew nothing of such things either, and even less about the confounding allusions to doom and destiny that followed. The prisoner's words utterly defeated the interpreter. He tried, but all that really came through was the image of a man digging 'a deep furrow or a trench'. It sounded, to white ears, as if Simon had merely garbled the old English saying about digging your own grave.

As Simon listened to the translation, a change came over him. His smile vanished. He turned his face away from the court, hoisted his buttocks onto the rim of the witness-box, and lowered his head between his knees. A few sobs racked his body. And then he started bellowing and howling. It was an unbearable sound, the sound of a bull with a sword in its heart, an animal with its leg in a trap. The judge paled, the court fell silent, the noise outside subsided. All who heard that sound were stricken, for it was surely the scream of a man tormented beyond endurance by apartheid. At last, the judge said, 'Please stand up. Please stand up.'

Simon accepted a tissue from the interpreter and dried his eyes. The judge asked whether Simon required a short adjournment to compose himself, but Simon pulled himself together, took a deep breath, and continued. In the next few minutes, he delivered as moving and powerful an indictment of white South Africa as has ever been spoken. 'I know,' he said, 'that a white person on this earth, whether he claims to be a Christian or not, all that he prays for, is that he lives for a long time and that he enjoys life. A white person does not pray to God that God causes us, irrespective of colour, to live peacefully and in harmony. The whites always talk of peace when they in fact do not exercise peace.

'I once feared a white person, M'Lord. I also respected a white person, and I also liked a white person. Even if I met a white person, a brown person, or a black person, I used not to lift my hand at that person. What I used to do, I used to break into places and steal. I never resorted to violence. But when I got to the stage where I developed the disliking of the white person, I decided that I should shed blood, that is, the blood of the white people. So I started last August. I went and attacked the white people at their houses at night whilst they were asleep. I did so here in town.

'M'Lord, I wish to state that I am a Christian. In fact, M'Lord, on each occasion, before I set out to attack these people, I used to go down onto my knees and start praying. Another thought came into my mind as to what I would do if the children saw what was happening to their parents and started crying out. So I decided, well, I should not touch the children, seeing that they really do not know what is happening on this earth. The children will be left untouched.

'M'Lord, I am not going to go into the details of what I did. The court is fully aware of what happened. Everything is recorded down in the documents that have been produced in this trial. In fact, M'Lord, I might state quite bluntly that I am not sorry for all what I did. In fact, my heart is free, and I feel relieved.

'White people like to kill black people in various ways. Once that white person is brought to court for trial, you will find that he has instructed an advocate to defend him or her, so that his life, his or her life, is saved. I disagree with such a thing. If one has killed another, he must come forward and tell the court, "Look here, I did this, so I must be executed as well." In what I am saying here, M'Lord, it is not that I am trying to defend myself or trying to put excuses of some sort as to why I did this. In fact, I am not to live, because of what I did.

'I have given the reasons that caused me to act in this manner; it is because of what I had witnessed happening to my fellow black men and also to me, because of all that was done to us by the white people. There is no fairness on this earth. One must know that as a fact, that in my life I have noticed that there is no fairness on this earth. So I must die, so that what I dreamed in 1972 be fulfilled. 'That is all I wish to say.'

3

Ah, Simon, Simon, your words still break my heart. There is such a terrible symmetry between what whites do to blacks in my country and what you did to us. And it is so simple to say that we had created the Hammerman as surely as the Hammerman had murdered four of us and that the entire tragedy could be traced to Dawid Malan and the law he formulated on the frontier almost two centuries earlier—the law stating that you had to keep your white foot on the black man's neck, lest he leap up and murder you.

Such a law fulfils its own grim prophecy; that seemed to be Simon's message to us. There was no hatred or despair in his last words, just clarity, which he seemed to offer like a man offering a gift—a gift of understanding, I thought, and a warning. And so, in 1986, four months after Simon's execution by hanging, I went to Empangeni to receive it.

The teenager at the wheel was a white Zulu. His name was Rauri Alcock. His parents were rural development workers, and he grew up in a mud hut on the banks of a river in northern Zululand, but that is another story. He spoke Zulu like a Zulu, and his role on this expedition was to act as an intermediary between me and the grave black dignitary in the back seat. Majozi Nxongo (pronounced *Nongo*) wore ragged khaki overalls and had huge holes in his earlobes, into which brightly coloured discs might be inserted on ceremonial occasions. In the white cities, where he had worked most of his life, he had been some white man's 'boy'. In his own world, however, he was a figure of great power and influence. He was the chief *induna*, or prime minister, if you will, of the Thembu tribe, a sub-tribe of the Zulu nation, and a guardian and interpreter of the Zulu *mthetwa*, or laws.

I turned to Nxongo for guidance because my inquiries about

Simon had dead-ended in a wall of silence. I was unable to find the cold-hearted Afrikaner who had supposedly torn up Simon's pass, but that was the least of my journalistic problems. I had been unable to find Simon himself. The Hammerman's tale had turned out to be something of a fable. It contained many half-truths and at least one outright lie. Simon was no orphan. He had a family. At the time of Simon's release from jail, his father was living in Ngwelezane, undergoing a witch doctor's treatment for tuberculosis. Simon, for some unfathomable reason, chose to deny him, even to his face. On the day they were reunited, Simon said, 'I don't know you, old man. Go away!'

Why? The black lawyers and tradesmen of Empangeni were eager to air their sympathetic views of Simon, but few of them had ever met him. Those who had—his family especially—would not answer questions. Some wouldn't even talk to me. Simon's cousin Sipho Mpungose, for instance, told me, 'Simon had a secret problem,' and walked away. A man who had grown up with Simon said he could tell me nothing about the Hammerman's childhood except that 'Simon never became human.'

It seemed I was incapable of even formulating the questions that might have elicited the truth about Simon. One day, however, a Zulu woman took pity on my floundering and whispered a secret in my ear. Her name was Mavis Khumalo, and she said, 'Simon was born wrong.' Her explanation was so confounding that I had to turn to anthropology texts for understanding and finally to Nxongo, in his capacity as guardian of beliefs I thought long dead. 'Something is hiding in this story,' he said, and agreed to come into the hills with me to ask those questions that lay beyond my imagination.

And so there we were, toiling through the lush green cane fields of Zululand in a borrowed Mercedes. Five miles outside Empangeni, we peeled off the tar and entered the Zulu reserve. We passed a memorial to the great King Shaka and an old Lutheran mission. Some miles further on, we came upon bus-stop number four in the vicinity where Simon Mpungose had been born.

As far as the eye could see, green hills rose and fell like the steep breasts of young girls. The nipple of each hill was topped by a circular cluster of mud huts, and cattle grazed in the valleys below. Otherwise, the landscape seemed deserted. There was nobody in sight save an old Zulu man sitting alone on the crest of a ridge above us. Nxongo hailed him, and he came tottering down towards us. He was wearing a tattered tweed jacket and a jaunty feather in his homburg. He stuck his head in the car window. His toothless gums clattered, and his black eyes darted hither and thither, full of curiosity.

'We are looking for the kraal of Simon Mpungose,' said Nxongo. The instant Simon's name was spoken, the old fellow started yelping and howling with outrage. '*Mtagaat!*' he shrieked. 'Sorcerer! That boy was a sorcerer! He killed the white men, who are my gods! I am getting an old-age pension, and he is killing the people who are giving me my old-age pension!' He flailed the air with his stick and hopped around in the road, cursing and laughing simultaneously.

'So you knew this man,' Nxongo observed dryly.

'Myself I am Mpungose,' said the old man. 'I was cousin to his father.' When Nxongo suggested he tell us about Simon, however, the old man lapsed into a muttering silence. His face clouded, and he stared off into the distance. 'I don't know,' he said. 'No, I cannot say anything about this matter. If you want to know about this matter, you must ask my older brother.'

It seemed inconceivable that such an ancient man could have an older brother. 'Where is your brother?' asked Nxongo.

'There,' said the old man, pointing.

Several hundred yards away, we spotted a man lying on his back in the tall grass at the roadside. I asked Rauri to fetch him, but the old man declined to ride in the car, so we had to wait while he made his way towards us on foot. When he finally arrived, panting, Nxongo asked why he was afraid of automobiles. 'I am from the time before cars,' he said. He and Nxongo started exchanging the elaborate courtesies demanded by rural Zulu etiquette. What is your clan? Where do you come from? Has it rained here? *Eh-heh.* I couldn't keep my eyes off the old man's bare feet and the geological accumulation of callus on his soles and heels. His feet looked like weathered rock or the hooves of a wild animal.

Meanwhile, we had attracted an audience. At first glance, this landscape seemed empty, but now people were rising up out of the earth and converging on us from all directions, drawn by the unusual presence of whites. Older men sat down alongside Nxongo, younger men formed a row behind us, and women parked themselves at the very limit of earshot, where they sat in respectful silence. I smoked two cigarettes before Nxongo deemed it time to get down to business. 'We are here,' he said finally, 'to find out the whole story of Simon Mpungose.'

Anger flashed in the elder brother's eyes. 'We do not speak of those people,' he snapped. 'They were the abomination of the Mpungose clan.' In Zulu, he used the word *nyala*, which connotes disgust, filth, disgrace. The audience fell silent and waited to see how we would deal with this rebuff. Nxongo was a statesman, however. 'We already know the secret,' he said. 'We have merely come to find out if it is true.' The old man demanded to know how we had found out. I said it was in the court papers—a white lie, so to speak, but it freed the old man from the stigma of being an *impimpi*, a man who betrays secrets to whites.

'Yes,' he said sternly. 'What you heard is true. It is a horrible thing. I will answer, but ask only the questions you need.'

I heard it first from his lips and heard it again and again in those hills. It was always the same story, told in the same way, from the very beginning, as all stories must be told. It always began 'in the years of the Great War', the war of 1914–1918, in the kraal of Bhaleni, a Zulu man of noble blood and an elder of the Mpungose clan.

Bhaleni Mpungose's kraal stood on a hilltop not far from bus-stop four. Bhaleni was very old, so old he could no longer move. In the morning, his wives dragged him into the sun on an oxhide. In the evening, they dragged him back into his hut. He had many wives, cattle and children. The exact numbers are lost to memory, but it was remembered that Bhaleni's favourite daughter was a girl named

Musa. She was about sixteen years old when the story began, and very beautiful.

Musa was the daughter of Bhaleni's old age. His memory stretched all the way back to King Dingaan, who ascended the throne in 1828. In his time, Bhaleni had been a great warrior. He was a hero of Isandlwana, a great battle re-created a century later in the film *Zulu Dawn*. To the very end—and he died a long time after Zulu glory had faded—he wore the *beshu*, the skirt of civet tails, and remained a fierce traditionalist. But it was during the Great War that the greatest misfortune came to Bhaleni's kraal.

It began when his favourite daughter, Musa, was stricken by *ufufunyane*, an affliction that became common among Zulus after the white conquest. It was a disease that struck only young girls. They would lose control and run amok, howling and hyperventilating and jabbering in strange tongues. Today white scholars will tell you that the girls were suffering from sexual hysteria, but Zulus themselves believed the disease was of supernatural origin. The girls were said to be possessed by demons—by the spirits of hundreds of whites or Indians. In this weak-minded condition, Musa was taken advantage of, and she fell pregnant.

This was scandalous. The Zulus were a highly moral people. Premarital sex was forbidden. Girls were regularly inspected by older women to make sure that their hymens were intact. Bhaleni demanded to know who had defiled his favourite daughter, but Musa would not name the culprit. In due course, she gave birth to a son. When the son was weaned, she fell pregnant again, yet she still refused to name the father. This time, however, the older women bore down hard on her. 'Where did you get this stomach?' they shouted. 'Where?'

Musa hung her head. And then she pointed to her own 'brother', Sonamuzi, and said, 'It was he; he is the father of my son and of the baby I am carrying.'

There is little to tell about Sonamuzi. I cannot even tell you his real name, for he was born under another, a name that cannot be spoken to this day. All that people will say is that he was black and that 'he was lower than a dog,' because only dogs and other animals have intercourse with their own mothers and sisters. Actually, Musa wasn't even his sister. They called each other brother and sister, as was the custom, but they were first cousins. In Zulu eyes, the distinction was insignificant. Incest is forbidden not because of the danger of deformed children but because it outrages the ancestors.

Now we must talk of the ancestors, of the dead forbears worshipped by living Zulus. If you are a Zulu Christian, your dead father becomes an intermediary between you and Christ. You pray to him as if he were a saint or an angel. And if you are pagan, you worship him in the old-fashioned manner. Either way, the ancestors are with you. They are entities that live in your house and hover over you at all times, helping, advising, punishing. Some anthropologists call them 'shades' rather than gods, because every man casts a shadow; it falls on his heels and follows him everywhere. The ancestors are that close, that omnipresent.

The shades command obedience to the traditions and laws of the nation, one of which holds that you may not take as a wife anyone within your own clan, even if this clan is thousands strong. You may not marry a woman from your mother's bloodline. You may not marry anyone from a family that has married into your bloodline, and, of course, you may not marry within your own family. Of all the degrees of kinship off limits to a lustful man, a sister or a first cousin is the most profoundly forbidden. The thought of sexual congress between a man and a woman so related evokes horror in a Zulu, because incest causes harrowing turbulence in the spirit world.

The instant a man deposits his sperm in a woman, the shades converge in anticipation of a new birth. They come expecting to meet honourable shades from other clans and to exchange mutual respects. If the seed has been deposited in a forbidden womb, however, the shades come face to face with their own kin, with the spirits of their own brothers, fathers, and grandfathers. This cannot be. Such a meeting drives the shades mad with rage: they wrestle among themselves and also turn their terrible wrath on their living descendants, on those who have subjected them to such ghastly indignity. There is little hope of forgiveness. It is said that the shades will hound the guilty until they and their entire bloodline are extinguished or until the world itself ends. 'This sin,' Nxongo told me, 'is the last sin. You cannot disown your own blood. You cannot cast off your shadow. Even if you try to hide from the shades, they will finish you. If you have this sin in your family, there is nothing you can do. It is better you die.'

A decade or two earlier, Musa and Sonamuzi and the child of their union would have been put to death on the spot, to placate the shades. But now Zululand was ruled by white men, and they would not understand why such killings were necessary. The whites would arrest the killers, take them away to Pretoria, and hang them. It is said that Bhaleni himself was willing to die in order to efface this disgrace from his bloodline, but he was too old to stand up, let alone kill anyone.

And yet something had to be done. Chief Mbango and his elders were confounded, for there was no guiding precedent in the laws of the tribe. It had never come to this before, because the offenders would simply have vanished from the face of the earth. In the end, Mbango concluded that the crime lay beyond his power of punishment—beyond any man's power of punishment, now that the whites were in charge. He washed his hands of the matter and left the final decision to Bhaleni.

Bhaleni summoned the father and gave him his new name, the name Sonamuzi, which meant 'sin of the family'. And then Bhaleni renamed his infant grandson, whose continuing existence was a hideous affront to the shades. Henceforth, he decreed, the child would be called Mkhonyoza, which means 'to wrestle' or 'to press with muscular force'. The purpose of that name, it is said, was to remind all who met him that he should have been throttled at birth.

Finally, Bhaleni banished them all from his sight for ever. Sonamuzi hung his head, took his pregnant sister and his abominable son, and led them away into purgatory.

After their expulsion, Sonamuzi and Musa wandered the hills of Zululand, homeless and unwanted. It is said that they settled briefly in Mhlabatini, but their secret was discovered, and they were driven out.

The same thing happened in Nkandla, in Mtunzini, and in Umfolozi, according to various accounts. Musa gave birth to a second son, who was named Amon, and a third, named Jonas. She and Sonamuzi became Christians and adopted Christian names, apparently hoping that the white man's God would shield them from the merciless shades. The God of Christians could not protect them from living Zulus, however. They were still unwelcome everywhere. 'Until the day he died,' I was told, 'Sonamuzi never built a house.'

After many, many years of wandering, Sonamuzi took his family back to bus-stop four. By now Bhaleni and his fellow elders were dead, and Sonamuzi hoped his sin had been forgotten. It hadn't. Everyone knew that the shades would ultimately exact vengeance. Tradition said that a man guilty of incest would rot alive. Nobody was surprised, therefore, to hear that Sonamuzi was holed up in a hut, his flesh decaying, his breath reeking of putrefaction. In due course, he died. There was no ceremony to bring home his spirit, because nobody wanted his spirit anywhere nearby. A few years later, Musa was obliterated by the shades. She walked behind a horse that lashed out with both hooves, striking her in the forehead. She died instantly.

So Sonamuzi and Musa were gone, but their three sons lived on. The youngest, Jonas, vanished in the early forties. The second son, Amon, mysteriously lost his voice, a sign that the shades wished to efface him from this earth. Amon was said to be infected with the 'sickness' of his family and to yearn only for the flesh of women of his own bloodline. Since he could not have them, he spurned all contact with women and became 'a mule'.

In the fifties, Amon also disappeared, and the only one left was Mkhonyoza, the boy who should have been strangled. Stigmatized

233

by his very name, he was taunted and scorned wherever he went. The people of bus-stop four called him 'Mpungose *impela*', which means 'Mpungose indeed, Mpungose both sides'. It was so bad that Mkhonyoza eventually made a jester of himself, introducing himself to strangers as 'the pure Mpungose' and cracking black jokes at his own expense. He drank heavily, had no fixed abode, and worked only to get enough money to get drunk again. 'That man was not well in his head,' I was told. 'Even if you looked at him, you could see he was not really human.'

For such a man, marriage was out of the question. He was once betrothed, but his bride discovered his secret and broke off the engagement. In the late forties, however, he met a widow named Colinda Ngobeshe. She had a child to support and a fondness for liquor, so she allowed Mkhonyoza to move in with her. In 1948 she gave birth to a son and called him Simon. His other name, his Zulu name, was Mnotho, which means 'plenty'. He was given this name, I was told, because life was good in the first year of apartheid. 'The water never dried up in the streams, the cattle always had milk, and the sweet potatoes never ran out.'

His name meant 'plenty', but his parents had nothing. The boy Simon was brought up 'like an animal', according to one of my informants. His parents were continually drunk, and he was teased by other children and even adults. 'People would use him for an amusement,' I was told. 'Truly, truly, truly, that boy suffered!'

Simon's mother died when he was ten or so. He was dumped on the Khumalo clan, distant relatives of his deceased mother. The boy's father seldom visited, and contributed nothing to his upkeep. Simon's peers, the boys who grew up with him, never invited him to participate in the rituals of their Zulu boyhood—never invited him to herd cattle or fight with sticks. They called him *umqola*, a term of scathing derogation meaning 'old woman' or 'hag'. In the stories they told, there was the recurring image of Simon sitting alone in a corner of the hut, not speaking and not spoken to. It was a Khumalo man who told me that he grew up with Simon but knew nothing about him, because 'our eyes did not meet.' It was dangerous to have truck with someone of Simon's background, because his curse might contaminate you too.

Simon was expected to turn out bad, and he did. When he was still tiny, the neighbours would come home and find him stealing food from their pots. They whipped him, but he was incorrigible. They sent their brightest sons to the Lutheran mission school down the road, but nobody seemed to care what Simon did. He was doomed anyway. In his early teens, he started pilfering from white farms. The patriarch of the Khumalo clan sent him away, saying, 'I don't want to see you here, because you are going to influence and spoil my children.'

The patriarch had acted too late, however, because when Simon left, he took one of the patriarch's sons with him. This was Mdadune, whom Simon later described as the only friend he ever had. Simon and Mdadune lived together in the bush, thieved to stay alive, and were always in trouble with the law. In the mid-sixties, Mdadune was shot dead while fleeing from the police. The Khumalos held Simon responsible.

The people of bus-stop four had not seen Simon since. They knew he had done a long stretch in prison. They were not surprised to hear that he had asked to be kept there rather than sent home. They were not surprised to learn that he had committed murder or that his very first words to his white captors were, 'I committed these crimes because I want to die.' Of course Simon wanted to die. It was the only way to escape the shades. All Bhaleni's descendants were being hounded by the shades, they said, reciting the woes that had befallen Simon's kin in the years since the terrible deed was done. 'These things are all linked,' I was told. 'They are definitely linked.'

Those old brothers on the hillside above the bus-stop were not aware that Simon had been executed, but they were glad to hear it. 'About time,' they said. Everyone laughed.

Towards the end of the trial, the defence asked Bruce Gillmer, a white liberal and a clinical psychologist, to evaluate the Hammerman's sanity. So Gillmer visited Simon's prison cell and talked to him through an interpreter.

Gillmer swiftly concluded that he was dealing with a man of superior intelligence. Simon had a logical, observant mind and a powerful way with words. His vignettes of life in jail were harrowing. His explanation of why he hated whites was lucid. 'I spent my whole life in prison,' Simon said, 'for things for which I should have spent a few months.' He talked of lurking in the dark sugar-cane, peering through windows in the well-lit white world from which he was excluded. He described the rage that overwhelmed him then and the pity he later felt for his victims. Tears welled in his eyes. 'I am not crying because I am scared of dying,' said the Hammerman. 'Dying is what I want. But when I recall all that happened, I feel very sorry. I am not a man with a bad heart.'

In the end, Gillmer could not contest that assessment. He told Simon's lawyer he could not help her, because her client was not insane. As a political strategy, beating white civilians to death was arguably irrational. But given Simon's experience, it seemed somehow understandable. Towards the end of the interview, Gillmer said, 'You are a Christian. Aren't you afraid you'll go to hell for what you did?' Simon looked him in the eye and smiled. 'Nothing could be worse than this,' he said.

Bruce Gillmer had no doubt what Simon meant. He was talking about the hell of being black in South Africa.

Or was he?

At the outset, I hoped Simon's tale would reopen blind eyes, but instead it offered an insight into the power of culture and the nature of blindness—the blindness of white men in my country. Some whites saw the Hammerman as a bad Kaffir who killed because he wanted a gun. Some saw him as a good man made monster by apartheid. Which was the true Simon? In the end, I couldn't say. I, too, was deaf, dumb and blind in Simon's culture. I could see him no more clearly than Dawid Malan saw the Xhosa on the far bank of the Great Fish River in 1788. In the end, all I really understood was that terrible scream, the scream torn from Simon when he broke down in the dock. I understood because it was couched in a universal human language, the language of pain. But what was he saying? The transcript gave no clear indication of why he was stricken at that particular point. So I obtained a copy of the official tape recording and had it translated.

The tape made intriguing listening. After all I had learned about Simon's world, his trial seemed truly farcical—less a miscarriage of justice than theatre of the absurd. The court was so *white*, so western, and Simon so black. Or more truly: so African. The psychiatrist who testified in Simon's defence was also black, also a victim of apartheid, but he was Indian, not African, and as culturally alien from Simon as I was. He reduced Simon's resonant dreams to benzine hallucinations and saw his loneliness as evidence of a personality disorder.

But I am straying from the point. I obtained the tape to find out exactly what was on Simon's mind when he broke down. These were his true words. He had just told the judge that he had decided to 'follow the swallows', to commit crimes that would precipitate his death in the manner so long foreseen. He continued thus: '. . . and I saw that Ay! No! It is necessary that I start now because everything is coming to an end . . . the in-laws, and the order of things, and their children, and the few pennies I had. I must set my heart and mind on the one thing only. I saw there was nothing I could do to prevent it. I would start a life of damaging things and others, knowing it was a path of no return. Where I am going I must open a furrow, so that when I look backwards I find I do not know how to come out again.

'All the time my heart was sore, because when I look at my forebears . . .' And there he broke down. His heart was rent open, and that is what was in it.

GRANTA 9 : JOHN BERGER
BORIS

Also
THE SOLITUDE OF LATIN AMERICA

- Gabriel García Márquez
- Mario Vargas Llosa
- Patrick Marnham
- Don McCullin
- José Donoso
- Manlio Argueta

Plus
Russell Hoban,
Graham Swift,
T. Coraghessan Boyle,
James Wolcott and others.

'An extraordinary story of love and greed.'
<u>New Society</u>

Granta 9 is again available at £4.50 from
Granta, FREEPOST, Cambridge CB1 1BR.

NOTES FROM ABROAD

Moscow
Patrick Cockburn

I left Lebanon for the Soviet Union in 1984. In January, the army had mutinied and the government lost control of Beirut, its defeat complete and unmistakable. The President held only his palace in which he was occasionally shelled by artillery in the surrounding hills. In Beirut, journalists and diplomats watched the battles in the hills to find winners and losers. In Moscow, the equivalent staging posts in the leadership crisis were state funerals where the coffin of the latest Politburo member to die was carried through Red Square. Surviving members of the leadership watched the funeral from on top of Lenin's red granite tomb while journalists and diplomats, standing in reserved areas just below, stared up in an effort to diagnose the progress of their various ailments.

There were four important deaths. Leonid Brezhnev and his successor Yuri Andropov died in the two years before I arrived, and in the next six months they were followed by Marshal Dmitri Ustinov, the Defence Minister, and Konstantin Chernenko, President and General Secretary of the Communist Party. Soviet officials, like hospital spokesmen, issued optimistic bulletins up to the moment that television and radio switched to solemn music. The death of Ustinov was first revealed after two American journalists went to a hall close to the Kremlin where the World Chess Championship was taking place. They found the door to the hall closed and a short note pinned to it cancelling the day's game. Curious to know why, they knocked on the door until it was opened by a cleaning woman holding a mop who said that she was doing the floor to prepare for the lying-in-state of the marshal who had died the previous night. Pleased with the scoop, the two journalists went back to their office but, worried by the status of their source, decided that since, like everybody else, the cleaning woman was ultimately employed by the state, they would attribute their information to 'a Soviet official'.

Despite all the secrecy, what was happening in the Soviet Union was obvious enough: the old order, the wartime generation, was dying. Soviet conservatives, the leaders who wanted to do things the way Brezhnev had done them, were weak. They needed a younger and healthier candidate and did not have one. The best they could do after the death of Yuri Andropov early in 1984 was appoint Brezhnev's old aide Konstantin Chernenko to succeed him.

White-haired, and gasping for breath because of his emphysema, Chernenko looked like a malevolent caricature of the old leadership and by the end of the year he had disappeared from public view and was meant to be resting in his dacha on the outskirts of Moscow. He reappeared only once in what looked like a bungled attempt by Soviet television to prove that he was still animate. It showed him standing upright to receive a delegation but obviously supporting himself by gripping the back of a chair with both hands. When the leader of the delegation tried to give Chernenko a bunch of red flowers he was too weak to take them. Twice he raised his right hand a few inches off the chair, but the effort was too much and the hand fell back.

A few weeks later I went to Chernenko's funeral, which was interrupted by a touching incident. Everybody, from the Politburo to the crowds outside the GUM department store on the other side of Red Square, was in a good mood. The leadership crisis was finally over. Behind me, on a walkway below the level of the square, special KGB troops, in their dress uniform of gold braid and Persian lamb fur hats, were laughing and smoking cigarettes. Then, as I was about to go home, Mrs Chernenko, who looked like any elderly peasant woman in a Moscow market, threw herself on the coffin before they could take it away. For a few minutes, the funeral came to a halt while she lay there sobbing.

Foreign journalists in Moscow lived in peculiar conditions. The government could never make up its mind whether it regarded them as spies, whose efforts to obtain information should be thwarted at every turn, or people whom it needed to cultivate and influence. Torn between the two approaches, the government tried both at once. The Foreign Ministry organized trips for journalists who, on their return to Moscow, read articles about themselves in the press in which it was said that correspondent X, far from showing gratitude for Soviet hospitality, had behaved in a manner difficult to distinguish from straight espionage. The pieces, so evidently based on KGB reports, were written in the pained tone of the trusting friend whose confidence has been betrayed.

Living conditions revealed the same schizophrenia: in 1984 there were some 300 full-time journalists in Moscow living in twenty foreigner-only apartment blocks in different parts of the city. The entrance of each was guarded twenty-four hours a day by grey-coated police who recorded the name of anybody entering or leaving. Foreigners with passports were allowed in, but ordinary Soviets were stopped unless accompanied by a resident. Inside, foreigners assumed that any word they said could be monitored by the KGB.

I lived in a nine-storey brown building, built by German prisoners of war in the late 1940s, opposite the Puppet Theatre on the ring road which circles central Moscow.

The building was divided between journalists and diplomats. The apartment next to mine was occupied by Colonel Miroslav Popovic, the Yugoslav military attaché, whom I often met in the evening as he left in full dress uniform to attend some military function. Three floors above me lived Antero Pietela, the *Baltimore Sun* correspondent, while the ground floor was rented by the *New York Times*. The authorities, in order to make foreigners highly visible, gave each profession a different coloured number-plate: red for diplomats and yellow for correspondents. In the expatriate community, diplomats outnumbered journalists by ten to one, giving day-to-day life the peculiar quality of a formal hierarchy, with the ambassadors of the major powers at the top and the nannies at the bottom. The nannies' life was not an easy one. Foreign ministries across the world, fearing that the seduction of the single diplomat would be rapidly followed by political betrayal, liked members of their embassy staff to be married, and there were therefore numerous children in need of tending. This was not difficult to arrange. One of the few ways a girl, just graduated in Russian from university, could get a visa to live in Moscow was to work as a nanny. Unfortunately many of the girls, more interested in Tolstoy and Turgenev than the care of diplomatic offspring, discovered on arrival that they had to work long hours for little pay. Discontent mounted and, in a development which would not have surprised Marx, inspired a movement of religious revivalism. The nanny of one journalist took to leaving written slogans around his apartment. One morning on getting out of bed he found a note in one of his slippers which read: 'Guard me, Lord Jesus. Satan is in this house.'

Social claustrophobia arose from the enforced intimacy of members of the expatriate community, and I escaped once a day by taking long walks through central Moscow which, apart from the six-lane highways built by Stalin, had changed little since 1917. Churches and monasteries, turned into offices and apartments in 1917, still had their primary Russian colours: pale pink, pale green, dark red and cream. Behind my apartment there was a long boulevard where almost every famous nineteenth-century Russian, from Tchaikovsky to Gogol, spent part of his life, commemorated by statues, small museums and plaques. After 1917 most of these houses were converted to offices as well, and the prominent Soviets who then worked there were also subsequently recorded. Walking along Strastnoy Boulevard close to Pushkin Square, at the end of 1984, I noticed a square bronze plaque representing an eager, bespectacled face; it was in this building that Mikhail Koltsov had edited the magazine *Ogonyok* (Little Light) in the 1930s. His name was familiar. My father, then writing for the *Daily Worker*, met him in Spain during the Civil

War, where Koltsov was both a correspondent for *Pravda* and an emissary of Stalin. Many of the Russians in Spain subsequently died in the purges, and Koltsov probably made himself conspicuous by denouncing informers in a series of articles in *Pravda* in early 1938: when he returned from Spain for the last time in December, Koltsov—whose face my father describes as one of the most expressive he had ever seen, characterized principally by 'a kind of enthusiastically gleeful amusement'—was arrested and shot.

To travel out of Moscow foreigners had to give two working days' notice to the Foreign Ministry. If you heard nothing, you could go. The closed areas included most places near the borders, the Urals, where much of the defence industry was located, the rocket-testing ranges in Kazakhstan and large portions of the Far East. When travelling close to Moscow itself, it was permitted to use some of the roads, but not others. I was frequently stopped on the road to Istra, a fortified monastery thirty miles west of Moscow built by an exiled patriarch of the Russian Orthodox Church in the seventeenth century.

Individually, none of these restrictions was very onerous for foreigners, but, taken together, they exerted enough pressure to encourage self-isolation. 'What is the Soviet Union? Upper Volta with rockets!' a journalist said to me during my first days in Moscow. At dinner a week later a diplomat repeated the remark. Over the next three years I heard the same nervous joke, mixing derision and defiance, a dozen times—reassuring, misleading humour that reminded me of Christians in Beirut and Protestants in Belfast.

Amid all this, I tried to remember that the worst that could happen to me was expulsion. I was in Moscow only because my predecessor as *Financial Times* correspondent had been expelled in retaliation for Soviet journalists, accused of espionage, being thrown out of London. There was obviously going to be another round of expulsions, but I thought I was probably safe because my paper had suffered the last time. Finally in September 1985, the dozen or so resident British correspondents were summoned to the British Embassy, housed in some splendour across the Moskva river from the Kremlin, and told that half of us were being expelled. I

Photo: V. Shone (Frank Spooner)

drove away from the embassy with Robin Gedye, the newly arrived *Daily Telegraph* correspondent, who complained sadly: 'After three weeks in Moscow entirely devoted to putting together the Habitat furniture, laying linoleum in the kitchen and trying to exterminate the cockroaches, I find myself suddenly expelled for impermissible activities.'

A British diplomat told me how, in the early 1980s, the British ambassador, believing that the embassy should have more contact with Soviet intellectuals, had invited 150 of them to the Queen's birthday party, the main diplomatic festivity of the year. On the day of the party just three of the intellectuals turned up. Even by Soviet standards this was on the low side, so the embassy drivers, all Soviets, were asked if they had, in fact, delivered the invitations. They admitted that, noticing that many of the artists and painters lived in distant outskirts of Moscow, they had wanted to avoid the long drive to deliver each invitation individually and had handed them over to the Soviet Ministry of Culture to pass them on to the appropriate intellectuals with whom the Ministry was presumably in contact. Enraged that the idleness of drivers had sabotaged his plans—for he assumed that the only response of the Ministry of Culture would have been to burn the invitations after putting a black mark against the names of those invited—the ambassador said that if this happened again he would fire them all. Under threat of the sack the following year the embassy drivers diligently drove to distant suburbs of Moscow and walked up long flights of stairs to deliver an invitation personally into the hands of each novelist, painter or poet. But the Ministry had a longer reach than the embassy imagined. On the day of the Queen's birthday the ambassador impatiently awaited their arrival but, looking around the embassy lawn an hour after the party started, he was disappointed to note that only three intellectuals had turned up—and those were the same three who had attended the year before.

Such incidents were misleading, chiefly because the lengths to which the Ministry of Culture had gone to prevent the intellectuals attending suggested that they might have passed on some vital piece of information, some key to understanding the Soviet Union. It strengthened the belief, notorious among journalists, that greater access through interviews and briefings from those in authority leads to a greater understanding of what is happening. In Moscow the belief was supported by the academic traditions of Sovietology which saw the Kremlin as a sort of spaceship hovering over Soviet society and exerting total control over the population. If this was true then the obvious, indeed the only, course for a journalist was to locate and talk to somebody on board, if not in charge.

There was some truth in this, but, after a few months in Moscow, it was obvious that the spaceship crew, far from being in total command, were trying with some desperation to respond to developments which they did not control. To some of the expatriates in Moscow these developments were superficial, masking the unchanging face of the Soviet state. There was also an understandable desire on the part of some experts not to admit easily to the idea of fundamental change which would deflate the value of their own accumulated knowledge. Russia has some special attraction to people who believe that Gorbachev is only a recycled Khrushchev and Stalin a replay of Peter the Great or Ivan the Terrible. It is comforting, since it requires no extra thought, to believe that we are simply seeing old patterns repeated, that all problems should respond to traditional remedies. A diplomat told me of an early adherent of this approach who had advised the British Foreign Office in 1917 just after the Bolsheviks had seized power. The western allies were worried that the revolutionaries would sign a separate peace with Germany. Experts on Russian affairs were consulted on how to influence the new leadership. Few had anything useful to suggest until one elderly official put forward a novel plan. He said that during his many years of dealing with Russians he had noticed their fondness for decorations. He therefore proposed that Britain award Lenin a knighthood and Trotsky some lesser but still worthwhile honour to encourage them to break off talks with Germany.

*O*n New Year's Eve 1985, Nick Daniloff, then *US News and World Report* correspondent in Moscow, and I went to interview the first deputy editor of *Ekonomicheskaya Gazeta*, the main economic newspaper, to ask him about prospects for economic reform. As we sipped tea and ate biscuits (invariably offered when interviewing Soviet officials), he beamed at us but denied that anything out of the ordinary was happening: 'We have discussions, yes, but we also had discussions about the economy in the 1920s, 1930s, 1940s, 1950s, 1960s and 1970s,' he said.

'Maybe not in the 1940s,' said another member of the paper's staff sitting beside him. Walking out of the office after two hours, listening to him deny anything had changed, we noticed a workman in the corridor removing a name-plate from the door: the chief editor of the paper had just been replaced.

The first deputy editor, on Soviet newspapers often the man in charge of the day-to-day running of the publication, was clearly trying to respond to two contradictory pressures. Even after Gorbachev had been in power for two years and Moscow was awash with glasnost, provincial officials balanced nervously between total openness and complete secrecy. Some found it difficult to get into the spirit of the new Party line favouring diversity of opinion.

*T*he turning point was the nuclear disaster at Chernobyl in April, 1986. It, more than anything else, proved to the Kremlin the impossibility of confining openness to only the peripheral issues. The Politburo's first reaction to the news of the nuclear experiment which had gone wrong in the northern Ukraine was to cover it up. Only when radioactive clouds were detected over Sweden and Finland did it admit that something had happened. The emphasis was on reassurance. Soviet television showed Ukrainian folk-dancers whirling about in Kiev as evidence that foreign reports of the accident were exaggerated. Ten days later the Ukrainian health minister appeared on television in Kiev to warn people to stay inside and to wash their hair at least once a day. By then you could go down to Kievski station close to my office and watch the arrival of trains from Kiev, packed with children sent to Moscow by the parents.

Gorbachev faced a political disaster. A central aim of his foreign policy was to reduce demonization of the Soviet Union in the West. He had declared a unilateral ban on nuclear tests to raise the credibility of the Soviet commitment to arms control. Now, as a result of Chernobyl, people from Finland to north Wales were being advised to avoid going outside in the rain. Worse, the Kremlin, by creating a vacuum of information about the prospects of Russians and the rest of Europe getting radiation sickness, made itself vulnerable to any rumour. Chernobyl caught fire just after midnight on April 26. By the following Tuesday the pressure for news was enormous. As I listened to the BBC World Service and read the Reuters wire, it seemed to me that doctors in homes for the mentally disturbed across Europe were assuring patients that, if they drank their hot chocolate and passed a quiet night, they too would be allowed to give press and radio interviews about what exactly was happening at the core of the reactor.

Late that afternoon I saw that United Press International was running a story quoting sources in Kiev saying that 2,100 people had died, far in excess of the number admitted by the Soviets. This seemed to me very unlikely and I rang the office in London asking them not to run the story, or at least that they print it in a manner that showed we did not believe it. This they did, but for the Soviet Foreign Ministry the UPI story was a godsend. Every time, over the next few months, they were accused of suppressing or distorting information about Chernobyl, the Foreign Ministry spokesman recalled that the western press had said that 2,100 people had died. By then they were in a stronger position to make denials. Ten days after Chernobyl the Soviet press started to report what had happened. The foreign press section of the Foreign Ministry by Park Kulturi metro station gave press conferences and briefings, marking the real beginning of glasnost on major events for the foreign press in Moscow. The Foreign Ministry learned quickly how to deal with the media. A year later I went on one of a series of press trips to Chernobyl intended to reassure Soviets and foreigners that everything was under control. It was expertly organized. In

Chernobyl itself, a typical Ukrainian wooden village twelve miles from the plant, bushes and fruit trees were beginning to grow in through the windows of the abandoned houses. The only people in the streets were soldiers dressed in military fatigues, their faces covered by white surgeons' masks. Closer to the plant, the soldiers were cutting down a pine forest withered by the radiation. In Pripyat, a town of 50,000 where the workers from the plant had once lived, gardens had been stripped of topsoil which was then buried in pits. Television crews rushed to film a clothes-line on which were still hanging an abandoned shirt and a pair of underpants, bleached by a year of sun and rain. 'The wind blew them down but I had them replaced,' said the Ukrainian in charge of the party. The press department was beginning to understand visual cliché.

*T*he months after Chernobyl coincided with the dismantling of most of the system of censorship. Gorbachev had started making critical speeches from the moment he was elected. Alexander Yakovlev, after ten years as ambassador to Canada, became head of the Central Propaganda Department the previous August—giving Gorbachev influence over the appointment of editors—and, from early 1986, new and radical editors were hired: Ivan Frolov at the Party's monthly theoretical magazine *Kommunist*; Vitali Korotich at Koltsov's old magazine *Ogonyok*, now in colour but moribund; and Yegor Yakovlev at *Moscow News*, a propaganda weekly for foreign consumption published in half a dozen languages and unreadable in all of them. Georgi Markov, head of the Writers Union for fifteen years and the man held responsible by many Moscow intellectuals for giving Brezhnev a literary award for his war memoirs, was kicked upstairs. In December Andrei Sakharov returned to Moscow after six years' exile in Gorki.

At first, Moscow intellectuals doubted the changes meant very much. In 1985, they had believed that Gorbachev meant only Brezhnevism without Brezhnev. Even after the release of Sakharov they would believe some reactionary article in an obscure magazine to be an indication that liberal reform was about to end. Their mood zig-zagged between euphoria and despair. Twice, when Gorbachev went on holiday in the summers of 1986 and 1987, every journalist in Moscow heard detailed stories that he had been wounded by an assassin. On the first occasion *Pravda* tried to disprove this by publishing a picture of Gorbachev standing alone and unharmed. Rumour-spreaders then countered by saying that the absence of Raisa indicated that the assassin had missed Gorbachev and hit her. Everybody was jumpy.

I went to see Korotich at *Ogonyok*, whose offices were now close to *Pravda*'s. He said: 'If we fail to rebuild now we'll lose everything. We must destroy all these stone and concrete people, and do something more human, more democratic. That is the only way to live in the modern world.' Given the difference between Korotich and the type of official with whom I had previously dealt, the corniness did not grate.

One day I drove to the offices of *Kommunist*, housed in a large eighteenth-century mansion behind the Pushkin Museum. Ivan Frolov, the editor, was surprised to see me. He said that his secretary had got the time of the interview wrong but, since I had come, he would talk to me for fifteen minutes. In fact, he spoke for two hours. I remembered that in *Under Western Eyes* Joseph Conrad spoke of 'the Russians' love of words. They gather them up; they cherish them, but they don't hoard them in their breasts; on the contrary they are always ready to pour them out by the hour or by the night.' Maybe the torrent of words was simply the result of ending half a century of self-censorship. I learned to be careful about the traditional warm-up question at the start of an interview because it might elicit a forty-minute response.

In Gorbachev's first two years, it was a comparatively small group of intellectuals and publicists, mostly from within the Party, who made the running. They were progressives like Georgi Arbatov, director of the USA and Canada Institute, and Yevgeny Primyakov, head of the World Economy Institute, commentators such as Fyodor Burlatsky and Alexander Bovin, and poets like Yevtushenko and Voznesensky, who had survived and in some cases flourished under Brezhnev without loss of all critical faculties. Progressive members of the party who began to be promoted to influential jobs in 1985 would not have survived under Stalin. A popular saying summed up the fate of senior officials who had lost their jobs under past leaders: 'Stalin shot them, Khrushchev sacked them and Brezhnev made them ambassadors.'

This new group of officials and journalists began to replace dissidents and diplomats as a source of information, even though many had learned their political skills as professional survivors during the Brezhnev era and were often tricky to deal with. The first time I met Korotich, he took me into his office at *Ogonyok* and then, as the interview proceeded, he began to peer around his office and open drawers in his desk in a mystified way. Finally he jumped to his feet saying, 'This isn't my office!' and explained that, as a result of building work, he had taken me into his deputy's office by mistake. As we moved next door to his real office, similar in size and appearance to the one we had just left, I felt a glow of sympathy for Korotich. In most Soviet newspapers there was no question of the editor making such an error, if only because his office was twice as big as anybody else's. In the following weeks I quoted Korotich's little error to friends as proof that here was a new and more modest breed of Soviet editor.

A few months later I met a Soviet friend who had just finished acting as translator for a visiting American. He said they had visited *Ogonyok* to interview Korotich, who spoke enthusiastically of perestroika and glasnost. The visitor was impressed but what had particularly persuaded him of the reality of change in the Soviet Union, the translator added, was a simple but significant incident. Half-way through the interview, Korotich had started to look around his office in surprise, then sprung to his feet and finally, with profuse apologies for taking them to the wrong office, had led them to his own room next door.

I did not resent Korotich's manoeuvre. He was a thousand times better than his enemies. Despite all the talk of the Moscow intelligentsia supporting Gorbachev, the number prepared to do anything about it was quite limited and of these he was one of the most effective. There was in any case, in the first eighteen months of glasnost, still a freshness and a sense of excitement in uninhibited conversation with Soviet journalists and officials released from past constrictions. It was also inevitable that this period would end. Interviews, however frank, netted less and less shockingly new information the longer glasnost continued. At the end of 1987 *Ogonyok* itself published a cartoon showing a fish in a fish-tank to which a radio reporter is holding up a microphone and asking: 'What do you think about glasnost?'

R eporting the Soviet Union was easy enough in 1984 and for the next three or four years. Journalists and diplomats who got it right were those who believed that something fundamental was changing in what made the Soviet Union tick. These changes had not started with Gorbachev and would not have ended even supposing Moscow rumour had been right and Gorbachev had been assassinated in 1986 or 1987. The new political atmosphere was invigorating but the opening up of society outside the expatriate community made the claustrophobia within less easy to bear. Relations between the press and the Foreign Ministry were now almost saccharine sweet. Officials now treated the journalistic rituals of interview and press conference with respect and saw correspondents as messengers not spies. I missed the sense of exclusion, of being a permanent outsider. It was time to leave.

Notes on Contributors

Ryszard Kapuściński is the author of *The Emperor* and *Shah of Shahs*. He is currently working on a book based on the time that he spent in Amin's Uganda. His last work published in *Granta* appeared in 'The Story-Teller' (*Granta* 21). **Jeremy Harding** is a translator and writer on African affairs. He lives in London. **John Ryle** is the author of *Warriors of the White Nile*, a popular ethnography of the Dinka of eastern Bahr-el-Ghazal. His book on Brazil, *An Unfinished Country*, will be published by Chatto & Windus. **Bruce Chatwin** was the author of five books: *In Patagonia*, *The Viceroy of Ouidah*, *On the Black Hill*, *The Songlines* and *Utz*. He died in Nice on 18 January. **Colin Thubron**'s recently completed novel, *Fallen*, will be published by William Heinemann in September. His last book *Behind the Wall*, is an account of his travels in China. **Norman Lewis**'s most recent work is *The Missionaries*. He is a frequent contributor to *Granta*. **Tela Zasloff**'s 'Saigon Dreaming' is her first published work. **Ian Buruma** is the author of *A Japanese Mirror*. He is currently working on a book on south-east Asia. 'More Fat Girls in Des Moines' is a sequel to **Bill Bryson**'s 'Fat Girls in Des Moines' which appeared in *Granta* 23. His book, *The Lost Continent*, will be published in September by Secker & Warburg. **Amitav Ghosh**'s most recent book is *The Shadow Lines*. His work has also appeared in *Granta*s 20 and 25. The poet **Hans Magnus Enzensberger** lives in Munich. 'The Extravagance of the Italians' is taken from *Europe, Europe*, to be published in May· in the US by Pantheon Books, a division of Random House Inc., and in the UK by Radius. **Timothy Garton Ash** is a fellow of St Anthony's College, Oxford. *The Uses of Adversity,* a collection of essays on Eastern Europe, will be published by Granta Books in the autumn. 'Murderer in the Family' is adapted from **Rian Malan**'s forthcoming book *My Traitor's Heart*, to be published by The Bodley Head in the autumn. Part One appeared in *Granta* 25. **Patrick Cockburn** worked in Moscow for the *Financial Times* from 1984 to 1988. He is now a Senior Associate of the Carnegie Endowment for International Peace. He lives in Washington DC.